Flight of the Silver Eagle

CDR Joseph C. Engel, USN Ret.

Flight of the Silver Eagle

By Joseph C. Engel SR

A Patriot Media, Publishing *Mini History Series*

First Edition

©2007 Patriot Media, Publishing

A division of Patriot Media, Inc.

PO Box 5414

Niceville, FL 32578

www.PatriotMediaPublishing.com

Cover Design: Patriot Media, Publishing, with contributions by Stephen Engel.

ISBN: 0-9791642-0-6

ISBN 13: 978-0-9791642-0-0

First Printing 2007 by

Trent's Prints and Publishing

Chumuckla, Florida

(866)275-7124

www.TrentsPrints.com

Dedication

Angie, I dedicate this book to you. You are an Angel on earth. Raising four boys while living the Navy life for 30 years is no easy task. It is your love and commitment to our family and our faith that has enabled us to share these last 70 years together. The tomato sauce, garlic, olive oil, and wine kept us alive.

We have been Pilot and Co-pilot flying together through the years of life.

Sometimes we had a flight plan sometimes not.
Sometimes we had a navigator sometimes not.
Sometimes we had great weather sometimes not.
Sometimes we had good landings sometimes not.

Throughout all the years we had each other, our family, our health, and our faith. I thank you with all my Love.

Joe
January 2007

Table of Contents

Forward

Writing an autobiography is in itself a remarkable feat, but for Commander Joseph C. Engel, USN (Ret.) to write about his distinguished Naval career and to have it published as a first time author at the age of ninety-four, is truly amazing. He is a unique Navy veteran of our time, recognized as such in the annals of Naval Aviation History. He is a Silver Eagle, Roster Number 171.

In 1916, the United States Navy began formal training for enlisted personnel in Pensacola, Florida, assigning eight Navy petty officers and two Marine sergeants to become the first recognized enlisted aircraft pilots to graduate as Navy aviators. Records show enlisted men flew as early as 1912, but the 1916 class was the first to receive the Navy's formal flight training. To qualify for training, the enlisted applicant had to be a Petty Officer (NCO) rate with an assignment in an aviation specialty.

The first enlisted pilots, designated *Naval Aviation Pilots* (NAPs), graduated in 1920, and were authorized to wear the Navy Aviator Wings of gold. Although accurate records were never kept before 1916, the government estimated that over 5000 Navy, Marine and Coast Guard enlisted personnel were awarded the title of '*Naval Aviation Pilot.*' These are the aviators called '*Silver Eagles,'* so named because of the silver eagle on the Navy Petty Officer uniform collar insignia, worn by the enlisted pilots when they flew.

In 1947, the Congress of the United States discontinued the flight-training program for enlisted personnel, but many of these flying veterans of the World War II era, went on as commissioned officers to serve with merit in Korea, Viet Nam and other areas of Naval service.

The Silver Eagle legend will live forever in Navy history and we are grateful for the service of these gallant men in defending our country.

Thank you, Commander Engel, and your fellow *Silver Eagles*, for your honorable service to America, and for your distinguished contributions to Naval Aviation.

Nelson O. Ottenhausen
Lt. Col., US Army (Ret.)
President, Patriot Media, Inc.

Introduction

The *Silver Eagle Association* (SEA) was founded in 1964, with thirty-seven original Pensacola area members. Captain William, F. (*Frank*) Cully served as the group's first President. Their headquarters remains based in Pensacola, Florida.

Silver Eagle Association members, 1964, Pensacola, FL.

In 1969, the Silver Eagles formed their national organization and in October of the same year, began distributing their formal newsletter, *The Scuttlebutt.* Additional *Wings* of the *Silver Eagle Association,* are located in Dallas, TX; Norfolk, VA; Jacksonville, FL; San Diego, CA; San Francisco, CA; Seattle, WA; and Washington, D.C..

Membership was limited to those relatively few Naval Aviation Pilots (NAPs), serving in the Navy, Marines or Coast Guard, and earning their Flight Wings as Enlisted Pilots. Detailed information on the history of the *Silver Eagle Association* and their membership can be found at the Pensacola, FL *Naval Air Station (NAS) Museum,* Buehier Library, and may also be obtained from the NAS Museums web site www.navalair.org.

Many of these *Silver Eagles* continued their service to America, some rising to the ranks of career Officers. Instrumental, enlisted NAPs early flight experience offered unique insight, shaping the course of the future for modern Naval Aviation Warfare.

Flight of the Silver Eagle is the autobiography of one of those *Silver Eagles*. Commander Joseph C. Engel's story is, in many ways, indicative of the sheer grit and determination of those early enlisted NAPs.

As a Navy Pilot Commander, Engel earned *Three Distinguished Flying Crosses*, and six U.S. Navy flying medals during the war. In the Pacific, as part of Fleet Photographic Squadron One, he flew constantly over uncharted territory through adverse weather, and fought off aerial opposition to provide photographic reconnaissance.

With the addition of his book published in 2007 at ninety-four years of age, Commander Joseph C. Engel, USN Ret. remains a *Silver Eagle*. His growing list of accomplishments is extraordinary.

Still leading and teaching others, Joe tells a witty, often humorous, historically significant story. A true Silver Eagle.

With *silver flight wings* destine to become *golden,* Joe and his bride of 70 years, Angie, remain active and alert as they continue on their historical flight of the Silver *Engel.*

Patriot Media, Inc. is proud to publish, and we hope you enjoy, *Flight of the Silver Eagle,* By CDR Joseph C. Engel, USN Ret.

Mrs. Dari Bradley CEO
Patriot Media, Inc.

Acknowledgements

Writing this Autobiography was very important for me. It allowed me to tell the stories which described my life. I'm 94 and still going strong.

A special thanks to my friend, Art Giberson, for providing guidance about how to get my book published and his efforts in making it happen.

Thank you Angie, my wife, for your endless hours of support, love, and caring during the last 70 years. You are an Angel on earth. I would also like to thank my sons, Joe Jr., Ray, Mike, Stephen, and their families for their continued love and support.

A very special thanks to my aunts Lillian and Mame Eichhorn who provided love and guidance throughout their lives.

The U.S. Navy gave me the opportunity to serve my country during a time of need, both theirs and mine. I am grateful. I would also like to thank all the men in the Navy I knew and who helped me along the way. Many of the pictures and graphics my son Stephen arranged, and used in the book, were provided by the U.S. Navy and obtained from their website www.navy.mil/history

Both the Pearl Harbor and Silver Eagle Associations provided a place to socialize and enjoy friendship after the war. They also provided Silver Eagle history, photos, and artwork used in the book. I thank them and specifically Silver Eagle Bob Buchal.

The National Museum of Naval Aviation NAS Pensacola has provided a place to go to enjoy the History of Aviation and meet old friends. Their website www.naval-air.org also contributed to the airplane pictures and Silver Eagle history in my book. I thank them.

Thanks to B.J. Miller Radioman VP-12 and J. LaMar Larson, Navigator VP-12 for their letters that were included in the book. I would also like to thank Harry Brooks, a friend and author of the VD-1 Big Book, for his support.

A final word of appreciation to the executive officers, from Patriot Media Publishing, for helping me publish this book. Their interest, hard work and dedication have been wonderful.

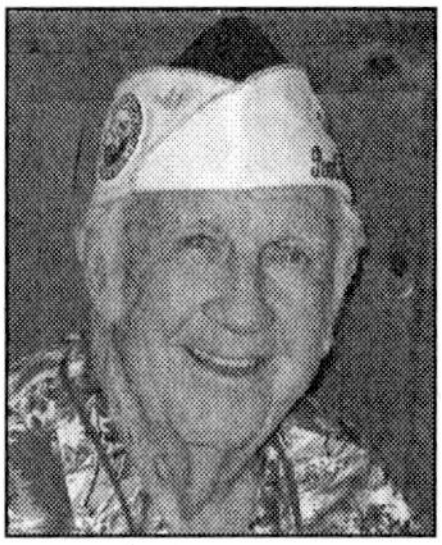

Publishers Note:
Patriot Media, Inc. is proud to credit the talents of Joe and Angie's son, Stephen Engel, of Symrna, GA. We were delighted to feature his wonderful graphic arts work in several places, including, but not limited to, the airplanes photos pictured on the cover. Stephen also helped his father and our design efforts by reviewing the manuscript, providing insight, photos and articles relative to the history of *The Silver Eagle Association.* We appreciate Stephen's hard work, photo arrangements and contributions towards the final draft copy and cover.

Joe and Angie's son, Mike Engel, Gulf Breeze, FL, was extremely helpful to our project from the beginning. We appreciate his early interest on his parent's behalf, and thank him for his continued help with the review.

Admiral Sherman presents LT(JG) Joseph C. Engel, with the Distinguished Flying Cross, February 1944

SOUTH PACIFIC FORCE

OF THE UNITED STATES PACIFIC FLEET

Headquarters of the Commander

In the name of the President of the United States, the Commander South Pacific Area and South Pacific Force takes pleasure in awarding the DISTINGUISHED FLYING CROSS to

LIEUTENANT (JUNIOR GRADE) JOSEPH C. ENGEL,
UNITED STATES NAVY

for service as set forth in the following

CITATION:
"For extraordinary achievement while participating in aerial flight as commander of a reconnaissance plane attached to a photographic squadron operating in the South Pacific area from May 8,1943 to January 23, 1944. During this period Lieutenant ENGEL anticipated in a total of seventy-eight day and night photographic operations and. special missions. The majority of these were carried out far over enemy held areas where he was exposed to anti-aircraft fire and enemy fighter plane opposition. On May 8,he made two parallel photographic runs over Munda airfield, where, despite intense accurate anti-aircraft fire which wounded his navigator and damaged his plane, he remained over the area and secured excellent photographs of enemy installations before successfully returning to his base. His superior airmanship and courageous devotion to duty in carrying out his missions contributed vitally to the success of air and ground operations in the entire South and Southwest Pacific areas. His skill and leadership were in keeping with the highest traditions of the United States Naval Service.

(Signed) W.F. Halsey
Admiral, U.S. Navy

Airplanes flown by Commander Engel

Naval Aviation Training 1937-1938

NS-1 by Stearman

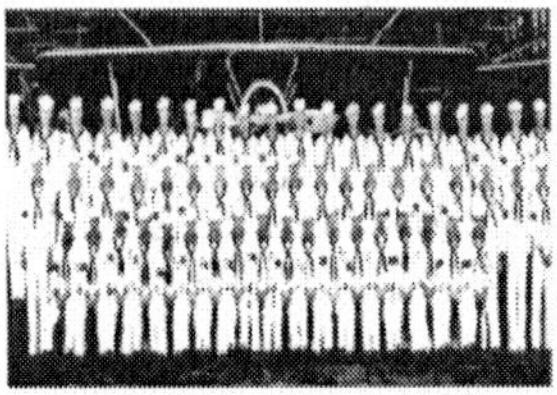

102E Flight Class 1938

03U Corsair by Chance Vought

N3N-1 Yellow Pearl by Stearman

TG-1 by Great Lakes

NY-1 Husky by Consolidated

F4B-3 Fighter by Boeing

Pearl Harbor - Midway Guadalcanal - 1938-1944

PBY-5A Amphibian by Consolidated

PBY-3 Catalina by Consolidated

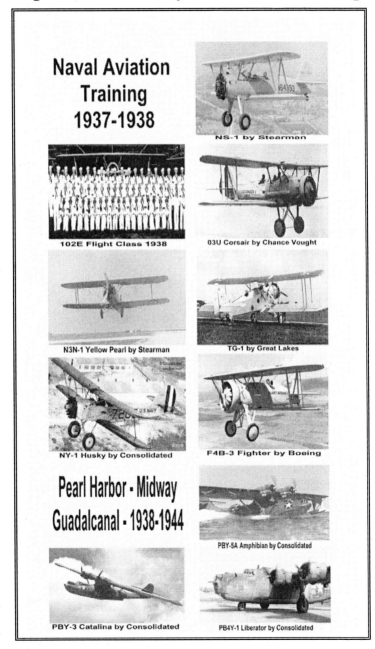

PB4Y-1 Liberator by Consolidated

Photo Training Pensacola 1949

F8F Bearcat by Grumman

F6F Hellcat by Grumman

FM-2 Wildcat by General Motors

European and East Coast Tours

SNB-1 Photo Trainer by Beechcraft

R4D-6 Transport by Douglas

R4Q Flying Boxcar by Fairchild

R5D-3 Transport by Douglas

UF-1 Albatross Amphibian by Grumman

R6D Transport by Douglas

TV-2 Two Seat Jet by Lockheed

Chapter One: Before the Navy 1912-1930

I was born on August 15, 1912, the second son of Louise and Henry Engel. My older brother, Henry, was born in 1909, my sister, Marie, in 1915, and youngest brother, John, in 1918. Both maternal and paternal grandparents were born in Germany, our parents were born in the United States.

We lived at 2425 Tremont Street in the Bronx, New York. The building had a grocery store and a tailor shop in front with two apartments in the rear and two large apartments on the second floor. My mother operated the store and my father worked as a bricklayer.

We lived in the apartments behind the store. We also had a 40-foot cabin cruiser and a boathouse concession in Pelham Bay, New York. The concession consisted of two barges. One barge had lockers and 200 rowboats, and we conducted our business and sold bait from the other.

I attended Public School 12 in the Bronx. Our principal was Dr. John F. Condon, who was later the intermediary for the police and the Lindbergh's in the Lindbergh kidnapping case. We lived across the street from St. Raymond's Catholic Church Cemetery where the Lindbergh ransom was paid. I played the fife in Dr. Condon's drum corps.

My first day at school was a memorable one. I bought a hot dog with sauerkraut and mustard, and a small glass of lemonade for five cents.

On the way home, I became thirsty and entered an establishment for a glass of water not knowing it was a barroom. I can remember hitching rides on the backs of trolley cars holding on to the rear light.

When the bricklayers' union went on strike, my father went to work as a conductor on the trolley car that passed in front of our house. At noon, I would get on the trolley with my dad's lunch and ride to the end of the line and back before getting off at our front door. When World War 1 started, we used brown sugar instead of white and my father went off to war. He joined the Army in early 1918 and served for about a year.

On summer school vacations my dad would get a job somewhere near the water and we would live aboard the boat. He would go to work from the boat each day. During the summer of our 1924 vacation, my mother caught a cold and died of pneumonia. Henry was 15 years old, I was 12, Marie was 9, and John was 6.

Shortly after Mother's death, we ran into financial problems. We lost the boat, the boathouse concession burned, and we had to sell the store. My father took us to his sister Barbara Steigerwald's house in Sayville, Long Island. She had four children of her own, Barbara, Frank, Adeline and Joseph. I can remember working for my Uncle Gus for fifty cents a day and wishing I could make the four dollars a day he paid his hired worker. We cleaned cesspools (now called septic tanks), dug basements, plowed gardens, cut and sold hay, all done with teams of horses.

Dad worked in New York City and visited us on weekends. Eventually he purchased the lot across the street from Aunt Barbara and Uncle Gus and started to build a brick house on weekends.

When we moved to the new house, my dad would leave early in the morning for work in the city, 50 miles away, and return late at night.

Henry soon joined him to work in the city. We three younger

children were left with little or no supervision for most of the day. Although we certainly had plenty of opportunities to play hooky and get into all other sorts of mischief, I don't remember that we ever did.

I can remember leaving the house one cold winter morning and the water I put on my hair turned to ice. My friend Kenneth's mother scolded me and sent me back home to get my hat, my rubber overshoes, and more clothes. Kenneth Philips later died of pneumonia.

With Dad and Henry working in the city I did most of the cooking. It wasn't good but we all survived. My father had charge accounts at the grocery store and butcher shop. I had an hour and a half for lunch and purchased the food on the way home at noon. I would peel the potatoes, place them in a pot of water, partially roast the meat during lunchtime, and complete the meal after school. It would be ready when my dad returned in the evening.

My sister attended Catholic school, and my brother and I went to public school. After school one day, I passed by the football field to watch the team play and the coach asked if I wanted to play for the team. I agreed. The results were my clothes were torn, I was bruised, the evening meal was late, and my father was very unhappy! The next day the coach said I could play on the first team. I told him I'd love to but I couldn't practice on weekdays because of my commitments at home. He agreed to this until the other players complained about my not practicing during the week. That ended my illustrious football career.

I graduated from Sayville High School in June 1930. Marie eventually entered the Order of the School Sisters of Notre Dame at the Baltimore, Maryland, Mother House. She took the name of Sister Mary Christine and taught in

Sister Mary Christine Engel

Rochester, N.Y., Orlando and Miami, FL, until her retirement to the Mother House. John opened an auto parts store in Sayville and after his first wife died, he married a West Sayville girl.

The Depression was on and no work was available. Two buddies and I met a friend in the local poolroom one day. He had just gotten out of the Navy and painted a rosy picture of the service. In hindsight, we should have asked him why he got out!

One of our friends knew a Coast Guard Captain who lived in town and he suggested that maybe we should join the Coast Guard. We went to the captain's house but his wife said he was at sea and wouldn't be back for quite some time.

We decided we couldn't wait and made plans to join the Navy.

We would meet the next morning at seven in front of the pool hall and thumb our way to the recruiting office in Freeport, 30 miles away.

At 0700, I was the only one there so I decided to go alone. The recruiter interviewing me said he was a second-class petty officer with 10-years service and that I could do the same. Sounded pretty good to me! I took the physical and written test and he said I would be hearing from him soon.

Somehow, I neglected to relay all this information to my father.

About three months or so, I had forgotten all about the interview. One evening my father answered a knock on the door and after a brief discussion said, "A sailor says you want to join the Navy but I have to sign for you because you're underage." Dad told the sailor he wouldn't sign and the sailor left.

Later that evening my father contacted my aunt for guidance. She advised him to sign because considering the state of the economy it would be beneficial to me. Dad was still hesitant, but finally agreed. Later he suggested we go down to the basement for a talk even though there was no one else in the house. He asked me if I knew about women and I said I did. This was my briefing on adult life and the birds and the bees.

Chapter Two: Navy and Married 1931-1937

I joined the Navy on February12, 1931. We traveled from New York to the Naval Recruit Training Center at Newport, R.I., via the Fall River Ferry.

Recruit training was very rigid, so rigid in fact, that seventeen of us decided to go over the hill (absent without leave). As I lay in my hammock that night, I asked myself, "Where would I go?" The answer was, "Home." But then, I thought, I can't go home and admit I couldn't take it. Particularly after my father had relented and signed for me to join the Navy. So I decided to stay. That was the best decision I ever made. The ones that left were given six months in the Marine brig at Paris Island, South Carolina, and a bad conduct discharge. Today you would probably get a couple of days in the brig and a lecture on why you were never to do that again.

All the recruits in my company took a test and the highest scorers were given their choice of schools. I was second highest and chose radio school because I had met another recruit in the poolroom who was going to radio school on the base. He had the radio insignia on his blouse and explained the Morse code dot/dash system to me. My dad was always against my hanging around poolrooms and on several occasions chased me out of them by threatening me with a belt drawn from his trousers. In light of events, I should have taken his counsel about poolroom advice more seriously.

At any rate, I fell for the radioman's pitch but it didn't take long to find out that being a radioman wasn't for me. I then requested Aviation Mechanics School and was told the quota had been filled. After school, I would be sent aboard a ship for completion of training.

The next phase was gunnery, shooting a rifle in an area called "the butts." The targets are at one end with people marking the hits and a dugout on the other end with people doing the firing. At lunch one day, the Warrant Officer in charge asked me what my plans were. I told him about my radio school failure and that I wanted aviation mechanics school but all the quotas were filled. He said, "How would you like to work with me out here in the butts until we get an additional quota for aviation mechanics school? Then we can slip you in on the additional quota." I thought that was great and thanked him.

I went off to Aviation Mechanics School at Naval Station Great Lakes, Chicago, Illinois, in April 1931. We learned aircraft maintenance (both engine and structural), wire splicing, wing and control alignment, and dope and fabric wing and fuselage repair.

Upon graduation in October 1931, I was assigned to Fighting Squadron One, based aboard the carrier USS Saratoga CV-1 at Naval Air Station North Island, San Diego, California, as a Seaman Second Class making $36 a month, a bunk, and all I could eat. I drove a gas truck and my responsibility was to refuel the aircraft after each flight. The squadron had FHC-4 Curtis Helldivers and made the movie *Helldivers,* in which Wallace Beery played. We played softball during lunch hour and Wallace Beery played second base. We all made money as extras.

In 1931 there were only 85,000 personnel (officers and enlisted) in the Navy. We had a flyover at North Island of all the aircraft in the Navy and the total was 150.

Squadron One later transitioned to the Boeing F4B-3. These were all-metal aircraft, designed before the introduction of aircraft control surface trim tabs, which were actuated from the cockpit. We had to adjust the trim tabs (aileron, rudder, and elevator) while the plane was on the ground. The mechanic manually set the tabs to allow the aircraft to fly straight and level with hands off the controls.

At first, we were finding it necessary to constantly reset the tabs, but after a bit of investigation we discovered that a seaman on night guard duty saw the tabs off center and nightly straightened them out. He thought all tabs had to be straight. Problem solved. By the way, sleeping on night guard watch was an automatic five-day, bread and water stint in the brig. I suppose the poor fellow was just trying to keep awake.

In 1932 the Saratoga made a six-week cruise to the Hawaiian Islands. We had to go to Lahaina Roads, Maui, instead of Pearl Harbor because of hard feelings between the military and the natives due to a military man accused of murdering a native. They later made a movie of this episode called *The Orchid.*

USS Saratoga operating near the Hawaiian Islands, 1932

In 1933, we made another cruise to Pearl Harbor, Oahu. One day they called for a working party. We were told to report to the quarterdeck at 0800 wearing pea coats and watch caps. We all wondered, why pea coats? We were in tropical waters. We soon found out! We were going to work in a refrigerated supply ship, handling beef, fruits, and vegetables. One worker asked if we liked apples and "accidentally" dropped a crate, which broke open. I assumed he was assigned this type of duty before. This cruise was the last time in my thirty-year plus career that I served aboard ship.

Squadron inspections always included a doctor and during one, the doctor asked me about my breathing. I explained that's the way I'd always breathed. He then gave me a note and told me to report to sickbay. The doctor at sickbay said I had a deviated nasal septum and I needed a sub-mucous operation and admitted me to the San Diego Naval Hospital.

After recovery from surgery, a doctor who put me on the Eye, Ear, Nose, and Throat Ward for a tonsillectomy examined me. Upon inspection after the tonsillectomy, the doctor discovered I wasn't circumcised. He told the Corpsman to send me to urology for circumcising. The Corpsman informed the doctor that there was no room in urology so he kept me in the EENT ward.

When I finally got to the operating room, they gave me a shot that deadened me from the waist down. I heard one doctor say, "Let me do this. I never did one before." The other doctor said, "I used to do it in (he quoted a figure) minutes, I want to beat my previous operating time." My confidence was a bit shaken but I survived and afterward walked back to the EENT and went to bed.

The nurse came in and wanted to know what I was doing in bed because I wasn't a bed patient according to EENT. When I explained, she asked if the doctor told me what to do if it bothered me. I said. "No." She said, "Put your feet against that cold wall."

One of my buddies came by the hospital to see if I was going on liberty. When I said no, he said that according to EENT, I rated liberty… another snafu. I think the doctors needed operating time (much like aviators need flight time).

After returning to San Diego, I was ordered to go on temporary duty at the foot of Broadway in San Diego. All the married men wanted this duty but I wanted to stay in the squadron. The powers-that-be wouldn't make the change. I found out later why all the married guys wanted the job. We were making $36 a month and the assignment paid $3.10 per day subsistence, plus you lived ashore.

The duty was in a warehouse and involved receiving food (meat, milk, vegetables. etc.) and putting it in an assigned space marked out on the floor for each ship. The ships would send in motor whaleboats for their supplies. When all the food was gone (usually by 1300), we secured until the next day.

On arrival at 0500 the first morning, the Chief in charge said. "Let's turn on the lights and do our homework," which consisted of taking three quarts of cream off the top of one of the 40-gallon containers of milk for our coffee. He then asked where I was living and when I told him I was at the YMCA, he said, "Why don't you shack up with some girl and you can have all the food you want from here." I didn't take his advice but I did take some milk and pies home to my room at the Y.

For liberty, I would go back to the base and play acey-deucey with the compartment cleaners. After three months, I returned to my gas truck duty with the squadron.

A seaman from the transport ship USS Chaumont visited our squadron looking for anyone who might like to exchange duty with him. He painted a glowing picture of trips to the Orient and the sights you could see and things you could buy cheaply.

It all sounded appealing to me. He suggested I put in an exchange of duty request and he would do the same. The request was turned down because I was a graduate of aviation general utility school. That proved to be very fortunate because I never would have survived shipboard duty due to seasickness.

One evening when I returned the gas truck to the garage, the Chief-in-Charge asked if I would like to get in the garage as a truck driver. This meant driving big trucks to Long Beach and Los Angeles, moving the aviation units' equipment aboard ship when they put to sea. It sounded good to me and I transferred to the garage.

In 1934, the Fleet went to the East Coast and they needed gasoline trucks and stake bodies. It was decided that the trucks would be driven from San Diego to Norfolk. We had a Lieutenant Commander and a Chief in charge. They arranged for our food and hotel accommodations. We drove 10 trucks caravan style for 200 miles a day, stopping for food during the day and a hotel at night.

Our uniform was dungarees and we carried a 45-caliber pistol. In Texas, an elderly gentleman asked if we were out looking for the notorious killer John Dillinger. We explained that no, we were United States Navy. He exclaimed that if he had known there was a Navy in Texas, he would have joined! We started talking about ships and had a hard time convincing the old gentleman that iron ships float. We lost him completely when we started to talk about flying fish.

On liberty in Shreveport, La., I met up with a lawyer and a prominent businessman. They bought the drinks and I got slightly inebriated. On a trip to the restroom, I pulled too hard on the towel rack. It came off the wall and fell on some dishes that were on the floor. Why the dishes were on the restroom floor, I don't know. When the hotel attendant came down, I told him I would pay for any damages I had incurred. He said to just be more careful and left. I thought that was the end of it but when I got to the lobby they ushered me into a police wagon and took me to jail. When I told them I was in the Navy and staying at the hotel, they called the Chief to come down and get me out.

After the completion of Fleet maneuvers, we drove back to San Diego and I returned to the garage and was promoted to Seaman First Class and a raise to $54 per month.

When the Fleet went to Hawaii in 1935, there was only one rate open for Aviation Machinist Mate Third Class in the battle fleet and I took the examination. I was told I did not make the rate because I made a grade of 2.89 on a scale of 4.0. I couldn't believe it. I had studied the book so much that when someone started to ask a question I could finish it and give the correct answer instantly.

I contacted the Warrant Officer in the squadron where I took the examination and told him I wasn't satisfied with the mark I received. He asked me several machinists' questions, which I answered correctly. After contacting him several more times, he suggested we contact the Executive Officer of that squadron. The XO said, "I know how you feel, Engel, sometimes I felt I made a better mark than I was given."

The incident would have closed right then if the Squadron Commanding Officer hadn't walked in and asked, what the problem was. After he was briefed on the subject, he requested the presence of the Educational Officer. He asked the Educational Officer where the examination papers were and when the officer stated that they were at home he said, "Go home and get them."

"I don't have an automobile," The Education Officer said. The C.O. reached in his pocket, pulled out a set of keys and said, "Take mine."

The Warrant Officer told me to wait outside and said, "Son, you had better be right because you've stirred up a bag of worms."

After the Education Officer returned, the Warrant Officer came out of the building with a thumbs-up signal. I had made Third Class. Evidently, there was some sort of illegal activity going on behind the scenes.

Upon making Aviation Machinist Mate Third Class at $60 per month, I was assigned as second mechanic on the Admiral's aircraft.

In August 1935, I was transferred to shore duty with Training Squadron Three at NAS Pensacola, Florida. On the trip to Pensacola, I stopped in New Orleans and ordered a blue-plate special for lunch. The "spinach" tasted bad and I didn't eat it.

I stopped again in Mobile to eat and the spinach there tasted funny, too. I concluded that all the spinach in the South was bad. I had never eaten collard greens before and had to develop a taste for their slightly bitter flavor.

On the road, I passed a sign: "Pensacola 20 Miles." After 22 miles, I figured I'd better stop and ask for directions. The gas station attendant saw my California license plates and told me that I had passed the air station. He said to go back two miles and turn left. I exclaimed, "You mean it's not on the main road?" The weather was cold and the hour was late so I stopped at a motel for a nice hot shower and night's rest. No hot water! The city boy from San Diego (population 150,000) was thus introduced to Pensacola (population 25,000).

I was appointed Plane Captain of an O2U2 Chance Vought. My duty was light maintenance and helping start the plane for student pilots.

We would crank the inertia starter and yell. "Contact!" The student was supposed to turn on the switch and pull the starter handle. Quite frequently, the student would forget to turn on the switch and it wouldn't start. After two or three false tries, you became sick with fatigue and lost your breakfast.

Later on, I was assigned to the night check crew. We made periodic 30, 60, and 90-hour inspections. Each check covered different aircraft systems components. The planes were checked at night so they would be ready for the early morning flights.

Shortly after arriving in Pensacola, I met a young lady by the name of Angelina B. Bellanova. Angie lived with her family at 321W. Intendencia Street, in downtown Pensacola.

The Bellanova home place on Intendencia Street, Pensacola, Florida

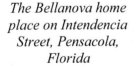

Whenever a sailor went out with a girl, more than two times his shipmates labeled him "true love."

Forty years later at a mortuary a voice called out, "Hi! True love." It was an old shipmate who hadn't forgotten.

Angie and I became serious and decided to get married on February 12, 1937 because I was getting $400 shipping-over (re-enlistment) money and it would go a long way to defray expenses. The church said we couldn't get married during Lent, so we moved our wedding date to February 6, 1937…the church could wait until after Lent, we couldn't! I borrowed $50 from a buddy to tide us over until I got the $400.

Joe and Angie dating, 1937

Joe and Angie Wedding Day, February 6, 1937

We were married at 0700 Saturday morning in St. Michael's Church in downtown Pensacola, Florida. We invited most of the sailors from the squadron. They had planned to kidnap me for the weekend but they got so inebriated they forgot the plot. Angie and I planned to take a 30-day leave for a delayed honeymoon that August to visit my family in New York and I went to work the following Monday morning.

Chapter Three: Pensacola NAP 1937-1938

I didn't particularly like flying because of airsickness, but I requested flight training in an effort to extend my tour in Pensacola. I knew that the enlisted flight class was due to start June 1, 1937 and acceptance took a year or more. I requested flight training on May 15, 1937. On June 10 (ten days after the last class started for that year), the squadron yeoman told me to report early the next morning for flight training. I told him to stop pulling my leg because I had just requested it. He said, "Well, I told you," and left.

I reported in early as requested and, sure enough, I was in the flight class. One of the students failed his physical examination on arrival in Pensacola and I was readily available for the vacancy. I phoned Angie and told her that the honeymoon would have to be delayed even more. She said, "Turn it down." I'm glad I didn't.

Flight training didn't come easy at first. We started in seaplanes on the water. On my first landing, I greased one on, so you never knew it hit the water and I waited for praise from my instructor but instead I got a lecture on landings. The next time I leveled off about ten feet above the water and it dropped like a ton of bricks.

I cringed, waiting for a chewing out by the instructor, but he said, "That's beautiful. That's the way to do it." The reason for the full stall landing is they wanted you to get the lowest possible landing speed. This promoted safety.

The instructor could talk to the student through a flexible hose, called a Gosport, connected to the ear part of the student's helmet. The only way a student could respond was to nod his head yes or no, which the instructor could see in the mirror over his head.

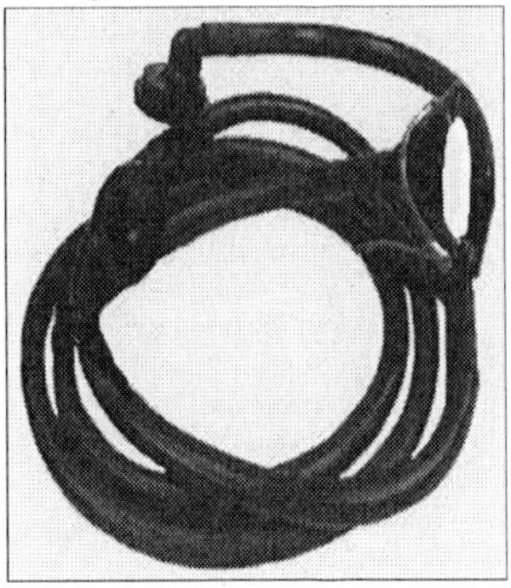

Gosport voice tube

After 10 hours, my instructor said "Engel, I believe you're ready for solo, but I have to show you how to get out of spins in case you accidentally get into one." After the first spin, I kicked the control stick and the instructor asked, "Are you sick?" He evidently saw how pale I was. I nodded yes.

We flew around for a while and when he saw the color come back to my face he asked, "Do you want to try it again?" I nodded affirmative. I kicked the control stick again and pointed to the ground. Once on the ground my instructor asked what I wanted to do and I said I wanted to quit the program. He said, "I'll help you if you want to quit or stay in the program."

"I want to quit," I said.

He took me in to the Operations Officer and said, "Engel gets sick in spins and wants to quit."

"Tell him what to eat and reschedule him for another flight," The Operations Officer told the instructor.

"No sir! I said. "I want to quit."

"Son," the Operations Officer replied, "you don't tell us when you want to quit. We tell you."

"I don't know what the policy is," I said, "but I'm not flying anymore!"

With that, he called a psychiatrist and made an appointment for me. It was an amusing session: The psychiatrist asked me if I loved my mother and I wanted to know what loving my mother had to do with flying; but he talked me into trying it again. I had no trouble on the next spin and my instructor said I was ready to solo and to get my hard hat.

The solo flight routine was to take off and climb to 1,000 feet, circle the short course, and land. On approach for my landing I decided I was too far out from the shoreline so I leveled off' at 500 feet and added power to bring it in closer. My instructor met me at the beach and said. "You had the hell scared out of me! I thought you were going to land 500 feet in the air."

On one of my solo flights, I went the whole length of the bay without getting off the water and taxied back to the beach. My instructor asked what the trouble was and I said I couldn't get the plane off the water. He asked how many RPM I was getting and when I responded "1500," he said, "That's the trouble, you have to get at least 1550. Park that aircraft here and take this one." The plane switch proved successful.

I also played football with the Naval Air Station football team. In spring practice, I developed a Charley horse in my leg. The top of the rudder pedal was the brake. I couldn't lift my leg to the brake without grabbing my pants leg for assistance. I decided to quit football before I killed myself in the aircraft.

Flying went smoothly until I transitioned to land planes in Squadron Two. I got sick and again wanted to quit. They sent me to the doctor and he took two big balls of wax out of my ears. That took care of the problem and I started to enjoy flying.

When flying fighter aircraft, all instruction was received while on the ground because they were single seated. One instruction for touch-and-go landings was; when you hit the runway don't
Say, "Thank God I'm down," advance the throttle and get out of the way for the next aircraft!

On one of my flight tests in fighters, I thought I could stretch my glide but my tail wheel landed in the restricted area. I was in trouble. My instructor, who was checking me from the field, said, "I'm going to give you a down (unfavorable check)." After walking about 10 feet, he said. "I know you can fly an up, so I'm going to give you an up and put you on report.

When I reported before the captain of the base, he said he was going to drop me from the program. I was stunned. My check pilot met me outside and said that he wished he had given me the down. He felt sorry for me.

I was in limbo for two weeks, waiting for what was going to happen next. I was finally brought before the Captain again and he asked why I had wanted to quit in Squadrons One and Two. Before I could answer he said, "If you think you can go through this flight training program and then go with the commercial airlines, you're wrong. I'm going to give you a 1.0 in aptitude and you're going to graduate."

What I didn't know was that there was a commercial aircraft with a four-stripe captain and a pretty flight attendant on base, soliciting students from the Navy flight-training program.

At this point, I should explain the role of Navy enlisted pilots. Naval Aviation Pilot (NAP) was the official designation used by the U.S. Navy and Marine Corps for non-commissioned pilots - a now extinct enlisted specialty. These men were carefully selected and trained and, because flying was usually their only assigned duty, enjoyed a reputation for being exceptionally skilled and thoroughly professional pilots. They served at sea in patrol, torpedo, and utility squadrons, and in air station utility units, ferry, or training squadrons for shore duty.

Eligibility requirements for enlisted flight training were relatively few and undemanding.

- Be a petty officer (NCO) in an aviation specialty.
- Agree to serve at least four years after completing training.
- Be recommended by his commanding officer.
- Be selected by a review board, which considered the applicants record and the recommendations of the commands, which had forwarded the application.

In the spring of 1937, while serving in Training Squadron Three as an Aviation Machinist Mate Second Class, I was selected for flight training (along with 66 other Sailors and Marines from naval stations and fleet units from around the country) and assigned to Class 102E. I checked into the barracks on June 10th and started the department ground training - the Flight Student indoctrination course.

The first order of business was organizing the class into two wings, right and left. A senior petty officer was designated Company Commander and two others were made Wing Commanders. These men served in their assignments for the duration of the course and were responsible for the routine activity of the class (such as daily musters, posting of security watches. and getting all hands in formation and marching to Ground School or to buses for transportation to the flight line).

Enlisted students were, for administrative purposes, assigned to the air station, but actually had no duties or responsibilities other than full-time participation in the flight-training program.

After "getting organized," we were introduced to the schedule for the indoctrination class. This was a two-week series of refresher lectures in math, grammar, physics, hygiene and (to our dismay) close order infantry drill.

Sailors are well known for their acute dislike for anything that smacks of Army life and we were certainly no exception. Of course, the class was required to move around as a group and the only practical way of doing that in any reasonable order was by proceeding in formation so we had a drill session every day for two weeks. By the time it was over, we looked pretty smart.

One of the most enjoyable assignments during these first two weeks was a visit to the Flight Clothing issue room. We were out fitted with flight jackets (the old style, Navy gray-green Byrd-cloth type), a Gosport helmet and goggles, a cloth helmet, gloves, and most impressive of all, a beautiful white parachute silk scarf about two feet wide and six feet long. The scarf, which we all started wearing immediately, was a flight student's trademark.

For official identification we were issued cloth arm bands and were required to wear them at all times on the station. Each of the enlisted classes was assigned a color. Our class, 102E, had the color red.

With the indoctrination course behind us, we assembled at the Ground School and marched across the station to the Pensacola Bay beach area where Squadron One, Primary Seaplanes, was located.

After lectures on syllabus, traffic patterns, and administrative details, our instructors were assigned. Then we traveled to the flight line (beach) for our first official inspection of our trainer, the N3N-1 seaplane. It was called the "Yellow Peril," because of its all-over chrome color and use by primary students. It was no beauty contest winner, with its uncowled Wright engine and skinny, round aft fuselage, but it was rugged and thoroughly dependable.

Navy trainer N3N-1 "Yellow Peril"

This first walk-around inspection with one of the squadron mechanics as an escort was for the purpose of acquainting us with the pre-flight routines, starting, and servicing procedures.

Since we were all aviation experienced there were few surprises, except the discovery that the rear seat instrument panels were bare with only altimeter and the engine gages!

Our instructors told us later (frequently and emphatically) that one could only fly by keeping one's head up and on a swivel and that the surest way out of flight training was to be caught looking past the instructor in the front seat to check the air speed or the ball indicator during turns.

This session also included instructions on engine starting and a chance to practice a start and run-up. The N3N was equipped with a hand-cranked inertia starter and the pull-to-engine "T" handle located on the right side of the fuselage just aft of the engine. Students usually manned the crank while the instructor, already seated in the front seat, set the controls and primed the engine the required number of shots.

The Wright started easily, which was fortunate as winding the starter up to speed was a real job complicated by an insecure position for the *cranker,* who stood on a short tubular step protruding from the fuselage.

When the starter was rotating at the required speed (determined by listening for the whine at the correct pitch) the person turning the crank shouted, "Contact!" The man in the cockpit turned the ignition switch on, replied, "Contact!"

In addition, the operator pulled the handle, which engaged the starter flywheel and the engine. If all went well, the trusty Wright kicked over, coughed a couple of times, then settled into a smooth idle while the man outside worked his way back alongside the fuselage on the lower wing walkway to the rear cockpit, climbed in, strapped himself down and completed preparations for a takeoff.

Usually, the Squadron One seaplanes scheduled for the first daily training period, were launched down the ramps on a four-wheel beaching dolly, with a towline to a tractor. This was done to control the launching, after which it was pulled on the dolly, up the ramp, after the plane was water borne.

To change pilots and for servicing between flights, the planes were taxied or sailed (depending on the wind force and direction) onto the beautiful white sand beach which skirted the bay side of the station for miles. By approaching on an angle, one wing float could be worked up to the beach, and the pilots could then walk out along the lower wing leading edge walkway and jump down to the sand, never getting their feet wet!

Fuel hoses for refueling were dragged out to the beached plane by the line crewmember wearing waders or swim trunks depending on the season.

After the final flight of the day, planes taxied to a low pier on which a crane was located and after maneuvering into position under the crane hook, were hoisted out and put back onto the beaching dollies.

The planes had a permanently mounted hoisting sling located in a compartment under the upper wing center section. On taxiing into position under the hook, the student (or rear seat man) stood on the front seat and caught the crane hook as the pilot maneuvered into position. After being secured to the dolly, the aircraft was towed by a tractor to the assigned hangar spot for maintenance or storage.

Students assisted in all the ground handling and on bad weather days, were assigned to maintenance crews to help with periodic checks or to wash down planes.

The Squadron One syllabus totaled some 40 hours, about half-dual instruction and check rides and the remainder solo time. A maximum of 10 hours dual was allowed prior to a "safe-for-solo check. In the event a "down" (a failed check) the student was scheduled for two rechecks. If he flew "ups" on these, he continued the course. If not, he was reviewed by a board of instructors and could be allowed additional instruction time with two check flights to be flown successfully after that. If extra time was not granted, the student was dropped from the course and, for enlisted men, was usually assigned duties at NAS Pensacola.

Simulated engine failures (throttle jerked closed, anywhere and anytime) were the order of the day and not many of us ever flew more than a few minutes without a '*cut gun*'. The standard operation plan was to shove the stick forward very emphatically, assume the proper glide attitude then concentrate on setting up an approach, which would assure a landing on the bay into the wind. These engine-out emergencies were usually carried through to an actual touchdown, which had to be a full-stall landing on the water.

At the instructors' discretion, sometimes to the solo check, spins were demonstrated. We were warned not to practice them but this did not deter the more adventurous among us, who then regaled the barracks with tales of their hairy experiences!

Students flew all flights from the rear seat and quickly learned reference points on the plane which, when positioned on the horizon, gave required bank angles and airspeeds. Practice landings were usually made from a 360-degree spiral with the engine throttled back.

The training area was the western end of Pensacola Bay, an ideal spread of protected water about five miles in diameter. A rigidly enforced traffic plan was followed, its direction around the bay determined by wind conditions with control exercised by observers stationed in a control tower located on the air station. Large fabric covered balls were hoisted on the tower to indicate the direction of the traffic flow. A "one ball" course was clockwise and "two ball." counterclockwise.

A recall flag was hoisted as a signal to return to the squadron beach if flying was to be terminated because of approaching high winds or bad weather. This system of visual control was dictated by the fact that there were no radios installed at the base or in the aircraft.

Once past the solo check hurdle, students flew another 14 hours, most of it solo, to the next checkpoint. More solos with periodic dual rides followed with power-on landings and steep turns introduced and practiced. After approximately two months and about 40 flight hours a final check was flown and the successful students, individually not as a group, transferred to Primary Land planes in Squadron Two at the Corry Field Auxiliary Air Station located a few miles north of the main station.

During this time the class, divided into two wings, had been attending ground school half a day, every day. The two wings alternated, flying mornings one week with ground school in the afternoon and reversing the schedule the following week. The intent of this routine was to assure an equal distribution of the more desirable morning flying weather.

Ground school was thorough and covered aerodynamics, engine theory and operation, aircraft structures, armament, radio operation, and navigation. Classroom work was supplemented by practical sessions; many of them conducted in the overhaul shops with actual work on aircraft in for repair or maintenance.

Engine operations included several weeks in the test cells where the instructors on engines, which could then be started and run by the students, could set up actual discrepancies or failures. Troubleshooting procedures were followed and when identified or located, the students corrected the discrepancies.

Radio operation was the ground school pitfall for many of us. Learning to receive code involved about an hour per day with headphones clamped over aching ears, listening to five letter groups sent by a veteran fleet radioman with a manual key. Half the battle was learning to copy, with everyone developing their own brand of rapid printing. Satisfactory completion of the course required the ability to copy code at 18 words (five letter groups) per minute and press (plain language) at 26. It seemed impossible but eventually everyone made it. Failure to pass the weekly tests made night school attendance mandatory and that is the only way many of us passed.

Flying at Corry Field was a giant step ahead in the program and gave all of us a feeling of achievement. The transition from seaplanes was surprisingly easy and most of us were soloing in the N3N-1 on wheels after only two or three instruction flights and a satisfactory check ride. Operating procedures in general were quite similar to those in Squadron One. A major difference was the extended operating area, with its complicated traffic patterns (course rules) and the very real hazard of getting lost!

After about 26 flight hours, we transitioned to the Stearman NS-1 and started aerobatics, three plane formations, and "circle shots" (precision landings to a fifty-foot circle painted on the practice fields). Landings were made power-off, starting from a point over the field at 1,000 feet. We were taught to make them using slips, and "S" turns. Either technique was used at the direction of the instructor or check pilot, who usually got out of the plane after the first landing and lay on the grass to watch and grade the rest of the approaches and landings.

As in Squadron one, every landing was expected to be a full stall…a three pointer. A satisfactory check required at least five landings in the circle in six tries—and most of us were hitting six for six before we finished at Squadron Two!

Most of the students who failed to complete the course washed -out in Squadron Two. A number of those we lost were victims of chronic airsickness brought on in the aerobatic syllabus (which consisted primarily of snap maneuvers—all variations of the "pull it back and kick it" technique. We learned single and double snap rolls, split "S" falling leaf, cartwheel (vertical reversement), precision spins and loops, pylon turns, and small field landings. The ever-present engine-out emergencies rounded out the course.

We finished Squadron Two with formation and night flying for a total flight time for the average student of some 80 hours. About half of this was still dual including the regular check rides every ten hours or so.

With an accumulated total of well over a 100 flight hours, we were, without exception, just a bit over-confident. Squadron Three, located on the Station field at Main side, was our introduction to service-type aircraft. (For many of us this was a rude awakening to the fact that we were still students with a lot left to learn.)

Squadron Threes' planes were primarily fleet-weary, two-seater scout and observation aircraft, the Vought 03U and SU. They were heavy on the controls and were not as forgiving of pilot goofs as the Stearmans had been. We quickly found that "shooting circles" in the 03U was different and there was still much to be learned.

We were flying now in the front seat and were for the first time permitted to carry a passenger, usually some line crewmember who needed to get his time in to qualify for flight pay. The syllabus was familiar, with emphasis on precision, and small field landings and engine-out emergencies.

Nine-plane formation, air-to-air gunnery, cross country, and radio navigation were new and challenging and an introduction to what we would be doing as Fleet pilots in the future.

Patrol seaplanes were next on the program at Main side in Squadron Four and on the same bay beach as Squadron One. The aircraft were T4Ms and PM-2s. Operating procedures and syllabus were similar to the routine we had learned months before in Squadron One. We paired off and alternated on all flights as pilot and copilot. On dual instruction flights, the instructor flew in the right seat and the off-duty student observed from a position behind the seats.

We flew around the bay observing the tower for traffic signals and were always ready to land "on the water, in the bay, into the wind." Landings were the familiar full stall from a 360-degree spiral started at pattern altitude of 1,200 feet. We were taught "flat" power-on landings, but they were to be used only at night or on glassy water.

Although these were twin-engine boats, they had no single-engine capability. If there was a loss of power from one engine, real or simulated, the rule was to cut the other throttle instantly and make the best possible landing, observing the standard rules about staying in the bay.

Another Squadron Four phase we all enjoyed was a checkout in the 03U seaplane and four shots off the catapult. This was a standard battleship-type catapult and mounted on the seawall near the station docks, which fired us out over the harbor. One period of night flying and a six-hour navigation flight over the Gulf of Mexico brought the Squadron Four total to about 55 hours for the average student.

Completion of Squadron Four left one to go: Squadron Five at Corry Field for fighter and instrument training. There was no doubt in anyone's mind. This was the piece-de-resistance of the course, the phase we had most eagerly anticipated.

Flying the Boeing F4B single-seater for the advanced aerobatic syllabus was the ultimate thrill and nothing I have flown since matched that airplane for maneuverability and response. It gave one the impression that it was responding to thought alone and that no hand or foot action was required.

Fighter training flights were scheduled individually, with an area and altitude assignment for aerobatic practice. Although the enlisted student syllabus did not include combat training, there were many unscheduled dogfights. This in spite of the well-known consequences of being caught: immediate dismissal from flight training.

Groups of students at an outlying field conducted precision landing practice in the F4B with a supervising instructor on the ground observing and grading each approach and landing. Landings were required to be three point; and we used to say "If it doesn't sound like a truckload of tin cans being dumped, it isn't a good landing."

During these sessions, if a student needed instruction he was signaled to make a full stop landing. After taxiing back to the instructor's position on the field, the student stopped and the instructor ran over to the plane, climbed up, leaned into the cockpit, and shouted his comments to the student over the rumble of the idling engine.

The final fighter phase, *Check-in-Five,* was an aerobatic demonstration over Corry Field. Students were allotted time slots (five minutes) with precise start and end times and altitudes. The routine included two loops, a slow roll to the right and another to the left, an Immelmann (a precision two-turn spin in each direction and a double snap roll in each direction). It was a demanding performance and a fine testimonial to the quality of students and the instructors that everyone was able to complete it satisfactorily.

The final phase in Squadron Five was instrument flying. Flight training was preceded by a Link trainer ground course covering basic instrument flying and radio range work. Flight training was under-the-hood in the rear seat of the North American NJ-I, predecessor of the famed World War II SNJ (AT6) Texan. Air work was a repeat of the Link trainer material plus unusual attitudes including recovery from spins. Radio navigation on the old four-leg, low-frequency ranges included orientation and low approaches, usually to the municipal airports at Pensacola or Mobile, Alabama.

On completion of these final flights in Squadron Five, we were designated Naval Aviation Pilots (NAP) and transferred to Fleet squadrons. There was no formal graduation ceremony for the enlisted students; just a brief meeting in the Commandant's office each Friday afternoon for all those who had completed the course during the previous week. At that time, graduates were handed their NAP designation with a handshake and a few congratulatory words. NAP's were authorized to wear the Navy Wings of Gold and we did, with great pride in our achievement.

The 1937-1938 Flight Class 102E graduated sixteen students, about 25 percent of the group, which had started indoctrination a year earlier. This attrition rate was normal for enlisted classes. We lost a few classmates through accidents; others were dropped for failure to make satisfactory progress in flight or ground school or for disciplinary reasons. Overall, we averaged a total of about 300 hours in our logbooks on graduation day.

EPARTMENT OF THE NAVY
VAL AVIATION PILOT NO. 7-38
is Certifies that
GLE, Joseph Charles
ving fulfilled the conditions pre-
ibed by the United States Navy
partment, is hereby issued a
tificate of qualification as a
AVAL AVIATION PILOT
for
ted 1 March, 1938

NY-1 Husky by Consolidated

NS-1 by Stearman

F4B-3 Fighter by Boeing

03U Corsair by Chance Vought

Professionally, the group acquitted itself well, with most advancing to the rank of Chief Petty Officer by the time World War II began. The majority received promotion to Ensign or Lt. (junior grade; jg) early in 1942 and advanced to Lieutenant or Lieutenant Commander by the time the war ended. Many were selected for regular commissions during the post-war years and served full careers until retirement.

The Navy terminated enlisted flight training in 1947 as a first step toward phasing out the program. When the first class of chief petty officer reported for flight training, through the closing of the program in 1947, 3,700 enlisted men from the Navy, Marine Corps, and Coast Guard earned their wings as Naval Aviation Pilots. The last NAP, Master Chief Petty Officer Robert K. Jones, retired from the Navy in 1981 after 37 years of active service. Over the years, the group, never very large to begin with, has steadily dwindled. Today there are only a few old-timers left to carry on the proud tradition of the NAPs.

Chapter Four: West Coast Tours of Duty 1938-1941

After flight training in March 1938, I was transferred to VP-7 at North Island, San Diego, California. Before reporting to my new duty station, Angie and I finally got the opportunity to visit with my family in Sayville, Long Island. Our honeymoon trip to California included a stop at Niagara Falls.

Arriving on the West Coast, we rented a small-furnished cottage in San Diego. It included furniture, pots and pans, silverware, dishes and linens for $25 a month.

During my tour with VP-7, the squadron made an advanced base trip to Alaska. At a stopover in Seattle, Washington, we landed in Lake Washington (a fresh water lake) and the aircraft settled six inches below the normal water line because of the fresh water. It took a longer takeoff run than usual the next day for the same reason. The landing in an open sea at Alaska was so rough we inspected the hull for broken rivets. We took 20 minutes to taxi into Woman's Bay, Kodiak, Alaska.

We operated from the seaplane tender USS Wright while there. On departing, we had to delay a whole day because we couldn't get to the aircraft because of a 40-foot drop in the tide. The aircraft was resting on the bottom of the bay and you could see the cable and anchor.

Upon arrival back to San Diego, we had to fly around about two hours because a movie crew was in the area filming. The scene being shot was supposed to be of a squadron of PBYs taking off for a flight to Hawaii but they were actually using our squadron just returning from Alaska.

One Friday in October 1939, after we had completed Fleet maneuvers, in which I was the bow gunner and master bomber on the Skipper's plane, I was notified I was being transferred to VP-8 in Hawaii and to report aboard the USS Wright the following Monday for transport. The orders gave me just two days to settle affairs and I spent the five-day trip to Hawaii thinking of all the things I should have done.

Angelina stayed in San Diego until I sent for her. She had to arrange transportation for herself, the automobile, and the furniture. We had to pay this expense because the Navy didn't recognize marriage below First Class Petty Officer. We lived in Pearl City and I worked at Ford Island.

We worked tropical hours: 0700 to 1300 with no lunch break. At 0700, the Navy sent a motor launch to Pearl City to pick up military personnel and returned them at 1300. They were picked up again at 1900 for the movies and returned after the showings. You must remember; our salaries were very low at this time. My base pay was $72 plus $15 commuted rations and $36 flight pay per month—and not everybody got flight pay.

The Navy had two 26-feet, S-type sailboats in the Recreation Department but it took four months to be checked-out and approved for the operation of the boats. A three-man crew was required. I was one of the few checked out in the operation of the boats so they were available to me most of the time. Bachelor sailors were always available to serve as crewmembers. My crew and I would go to the recreation area, rig the sailboat, sail over to Pearl City, and pick up Angie. She brought the sandwiches and cold drinks and we would sail all afternoon.

The small house Angie and I rented was owned by a Japanese couple, and they had a 5 years old grandson who visited us frequently. It seems odd but now I remember him showing us some Japanese comic books where planes were dropping bombs on people and he said the planes were Japanese and the people were Americans. I never imagined that those comic books were actually a preview of what would happen on December 7, 1941.

Our son, Joseph Jr., was born in Capulauney Hospital on March 27, 1940. On the way to the hospital Angie started having labor pains and asked me to hurry; when they subsided, she said, "You're going too fast!" We got to the hospital in fits and starts.

Joe, Joe Jr., and Angie at home in Pearl City, Hawaii, 1940

My Aunt Lillian visited us shortly after Joe was born and we all went to John Rogers Airport. I asked the manager if I could rent a plane. He asked if I had a license and I told him I was a Navy pilot but I would need a check out because it had been quite some time since I had flown light planes. The check plane was a side-by-side cockpit with a push-pull throttle. The plane was so light I had trouble landing because it floated and I didn't feel comfortable in it. I asked for a check in another plane that had a fore and aft cockpit similar to a Navy trainer. I felt comfortable in this plane and asked for another helmet so I could take my aunt for a ride.

After 15 or 20 minutes of sight seeing I landed and told my wife to get in the rear seat.

"I have to take care of the baby," She said. She was reluctant to go because she had never been flying before. Just before take-off, she stood up and asked where her parachute was. I said. "You wouldn't know how to use it if you had one."

The entire cost of the whole operation was less than $10.00. I told the manager I thought it was a real bargain and he invited me back and even furnished me with a civilian flying license, which I still have.

Joe flying as NAP copilot in lead aircraft.

At the time, John Rogers was a grass field at the end of a dirt road; now it is an international airport. I always wished that I had a picture of the aircraft and me.

The one downside to the initial Naval Aviation Pilot program was NAPs were not allowed to become aircraft commanders; however, we could, and did, serve as co-pilots or navigators. Later the rule changed.

I was the Skipper's co-pilot and on each flight he would say, "Engel put up the blind flying hood." I asked him if he desired to fly instruments and he would say "no."

One day we had a squadron beer party and I got up enough nerve to ask him why he put me under the hood all the time as I thought I was a pretty fair instrument pilot. He said, "If you stop eating that garlic you won't go under the hood!" I then told my darling Italian Angelina to stop feeding me garlic unless I had 30 days leave because I wanted to see what Honolulu looked like from the air!

After one flight, I told the Skipper I went through the same flight training as he had, but I hadn't made a landing in eight months. He said, "Son, I only fly four hours a month and when I do I make the landings." I felt let down but about two weeks later I was scheduled to fly with a cadet and he asked if I wanted to make a landing. Of course, I said, "Yes." I later learned he was ordered to let me make landings until I got tired. My questioning the Skipper paid off.

We made an advanced base trip to Midway where two other PBY squadrons were moored in the lagoon. All the officers went aboard the seaplane tender. A skeleton crew of mechanic, radioman, and an enlisted pilot remained aboard the aircraft. That evening the radioman said, "I just received a blinker message from the ship ordering us to move to buoy number one." I told him to jig the message (request confirmation) because I wasn't allowed to taxi the aircraft by myself in the daytime, let alone at night, in the middle of 24 aircraft with only their running lights on. He jigged the message and the answer was to move.

I told the chief mechanic (plane captain) to single up the mooring line and go to the tower to help start the engines, and told the radioman to go to the after hatch with the sea anchor (this retards the aircraft's speed). After the engines were started, the Chief went to the bow with a flashlight, cast off the bowline and looked for the number one buoy. I didn't breathe a sigh of relief until we were safely secured to the buoy. The next morning when the Skipper came aboard he remarked, "We weren't moored here yesterday, were we?"

I told him the events of the previous evening and he said, "They moved the wrong aircraft!" A commissioned officer was aboard the aircraft, which was to be moved. At quarters on return to Pearl Harbor, the Skipper commended me for successfully moving the aircraft.

We received orders to undertake a refueling practice with a submarine in the Pacific Ocean. The object was to land, refuel from the submarine, and take off. Landing and taking off in heavy seas was no easy task. When we arrived at the submarine, the Skipper went aboard for coffee while we refueled the aircraft. The task is accomplished by pulling the gas hose through the salt water and then clearing the salt water from the hose by running about five gallons of fuel overboard. The fuel was filtered through a chamois into the plane's tanks.

The Skipper announced that we were going to have some congressional representatives and high-ranking officers visiting us soon. They wanted us to fly them over to Kaneohe Bay lagoon to survey the feasibility of establishing a naval air station there. The Skipper said he didn't think it would happen. The guests came, we landed in the lagoon, they surveyed the area and eventually built the air station: NAS Kaneohe Bay. We were the first squadron aboard because our skipper was the senior skipper of Patrol Wing One. NAS Pearl Harbor was Patrol Wing Two. We also changed our squadron designation from VP-24 to VP-12.

I was an Aircraft Mechanic First Class with a Naval Aviation Pilot's designation. Instead, it was my desire to become an aircraft commander. To accomplish that goal, I needed a commission. The first steps to becoming a commissioned officer were to pass the Chief and Warrant Officer Exams. Angie wanted to visit her parents in Pensacola to show off 16-month-old Joe and I used her three-month absence to study hard.

The Skipper was very cooperative. He told me to check the flight schedule and if I wasn't on it, I could go back to the barracks and study. I took the examination for Chief Aviation Machinist Mate in September 1941 and for Warrant Officer that October.

The written Warrant examination took seven days: You had to present an autobiography of your life and demonstrate expertise in shipboard engineering including knowledge of superheated steam engines, refrigeration, oil pumps, and air compressors. There was also a seven-day practical examination which included drilling a company of Marines, turning out a keyway on a lathe and milling machine, and the overhaul and timing of aircraft engines.

Angie and Joe Junior returned to Hawaii in September 1941 and in October we flew, our old PBY-3s back to San Diego and got new amphibious type PBY-5As from Consolidated Aircraft Corporation to fly back. The trip took 19 hours to the States and 21 hours on the return leg.

PBY-3 Catalina by Consolidated

PBY-5A Amphibian by Consolidated

I was baby-sitting one day while Angie was shopping at the commissary when my buddy Lloyd "Windy" Tracy dropped in. Joe Junior's hair was little golden ringlets and Windy had the brilliant idea that we give him a "butch" haircut. Angie cried and cried when she saw little Joe. Windy and I spent a good deal of time in the doghouse. One good thing came of the incident: I named my aircraft "Butch."

"Butch"

State of Hawaii Certificate of Competency issued for private pilots.

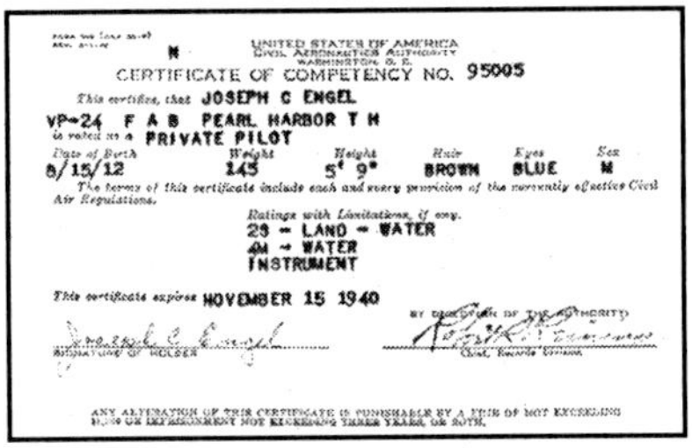

UNITED STATES OF AMERICA
CIVIL AERONAUTICS AUTHORITY
WASHINGTON, D. C.

CERTIFICATE OF COMPETENCY NO. 95005

This certifies, that JOSEPH C ENGEL
VP-24 F A B PEARL HARBOR T H
is rated as a PRIVATE PILOT

Date of Birth	Weight	Height	Hair	Eyes	Sex
8/15/12	145	5' 9"	BROWN	BLUE	M

The terms of this certificate include each and every provision of the currently effective Civil Air Regulations.

Ratings with Limitations, if any.
2S - LAND - WATER
4M - WATER
INSTRUMENT

This certificate expires NOVEMBER 15 1940

Signature of Holder — By direction of the Authority, Chief, Records Division

ANY ALTERATION OF THIS CERTIFICATE IS PUNISHABLE BY A FINE OF NOT EXCEEDING $1,000 OR IMPRISONMENT NOT EXCEEDING THREE YEARS, OR BOTH.

Joe Engel - 1941

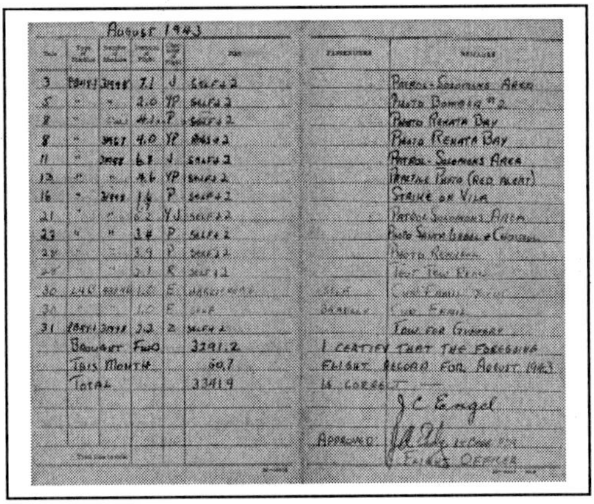

August 1943

3	PB4Y-1	3998	7.1	J	Self + 2		Patrol - Solomons Area
5	"	"	2.0	YP	Self + 2		Photo Bombing #2
8	"	[illegible]	4.1	P	Self + 2		Photo Rekata Bay
8	"	3967	4.0	YP	[illegible] + 2		Photo Rekata Bay
11	"	3988	6.8	J	Self + 2		Patrol - Solomons Area
13	"	"	4.6	YP	Self + 2		Practice Photo (Red Alert)
16	"	3999	1.6	P	Self + 2		Strike on Vila
21	"	"	6.2	YJ	Self + 2		Patrol Solomons Area
23	"	"	3.8	P	Self + 2		Photo Santa Isabel & Choiseul
28	"	"	3.9	P	Self + 2		Photo [illegible]
[illegible]		"	2.1	R	Self + 2		[illegible]
30	[illegible]	[illegible]	1.0	E	[illegible]	[illegible]	[illegible]
30			1.0	E	[illegible]	[illegible]	[illegible]
31	PB4Y-1	3998	2.2	Z	Self + 2		Tow for Gunnery
	Brought Fwd		3291.2				
	This Month		50.7				
	Total		3341.9				

I certify that the foregoing flight record for August 1943 is correct.
J C Engel
Approved [signature] Flight Officer

Flight Log, Midway 1943

Inside the PB4Y Cockpit

Chapter Five: *WAR!* Pearl Harbor Attack 1941-1944

We were enjoying our tour in Hawaii and requested an extension but unfortunate world events changed our plans. On Sunday morning December 7, 1941, we left our house for church, which was just outside the main gate. We said hello to our next-door neighbor who was going down to the squadron to paint and repair his son's bicycle for Christmas. After leaving church we could see the bombing and strafing of our hangars. The Marine at the main gate shouted, "You're not going to bring your family in here, can't you see we're under attack?"

Dark plumes of smoke from Battleship Row loom over shops and storage buildings at Pearl Harbor, December 7, 1941, making it nearly impossible for the Engel family to return to their quarters.

I told Angie to go to the beach and stay there until it was over. She took the car and rushed to our quarters on the base to get some blankets and food before going to the beach and I headed for the hangar.

On the way down, I was intercepted by an officer and told to report to the armory. Once there, I was provided a 30-caliber rifle, ammunition, and a 1918 vintage metal helmet. The helmet came in two boxes: one box had the metal helmet and the other had the leather liner with attaching screws. I never did figure out how to assemble the helmet. The rifle, and my marksmanship, were not very effective either, but I survived the strafing and bombing.

PBY patrol planes go up in flames at Kaneohe Bay Naval Air Station after being bombed by Japanese bombers, December 7, 1941

Our neighbor, Dale S. (Chubby) Lyons, had his leg blown off but he returned to active duty as a pilot and carrier qualified despite having an artificial leg.

After things settled down we found all our aircraft and hangars were either destroyed or damaged. We were told to go to the mess hall and put our white uniforms in the coffee urn to turn them brown because whites were too conspicuous from the air. I borrowed a shirt and trousers from a Marine to keep from putting on wet clothes. Then we set up a defense on the hill with machine guns from the armory and those salvaged from damaged aircraft as a defense against future attacks.

Later that night they read off a list of names (mine was included) and we were told to try to get some sleep, because we were going to be bussed over to Pearl Harbor the next morning for patrol duty. Before going to sleep that night I said to myself, "We have our Fleet and Army Air Force at Pearl and we will retaliate in the morning." Little did I know the status of these units!

When we arrived at the Fleet landing at Pearl Harbor, I couldn't believe my eyes. Everything appeared to be on fire, oil was about three feet deep on the water, ships were upside down, motor boats and motor launches were floating about aimlessly with no one in them. A few boats were manned by service members searching for survivors.

While we slept on cots in the hangar under aircraft, which were being repaired and armed for take off the next morning, we found they'd repaired the holes on the bottoms of the aircraft so they wouldn't sink. However, they missed some of the holes on the tops, which created a strange noise from the wind.

We couldn't get the wing tip floats up, so we went on the 14-hour search with them down.

When we got back to the base that night, we had no radio guidance and the only illumination was two florescent lights, one vertical, and the other a V. You had to line them up like a gunsight and land in the channel. On approach, we were met by gunfire from confused American gunners.

While some boats drifted aimlessly, others searched the oil-soaked water for survivors

We discovered that the reason our floats wouldn't go up was because a bullet was lodged in the worm gear.

The Monday following the air raid, my wife and son attended the funeral of squadron personnel killed in the attack. VP-11 lost seven, VP- 12, nine, VP-14, one, NAS one, and one civilian. Ninety-seven men were wounded.

One Japanese aircraft crashed on the base. The pilot was Lieutenant Lida, the flight leader. He was buried in an adjacent grave with the 18 other downed Japanese flyers.

CPO John Finn

Chief Petty Officer, John William Finn, was awarded the Medal of Honor for heroic services, and a Purple Heart for being wounded that day.

After three weeks of patrol at Pearl, I returned to Kaneohe and my family. I had had no communication with Angie and Joe throughout that three-week period. I immediately requested air transportation back to the States for my family because of Japanese submarines in the area. Our living status changed considerably.

We had to paint our windows black so no lights could to be seen from the outside and all automobile headlights were painted except for an area in the center about the size of a half dollar. When the air raid sounded, all dependents were required to go to the air raid shelter. My son's first words were, "Air raid, Mama!"

Years after I had retired I wrote an article about Pearl Harbor for the NAP periodical *The Scuttlebutt* and received a letter from a shipmate of that period.

B.J. Miller
Aurora, CO 80010
7 November 1991

Dear Joe,

I doubt if you remember me. I was second radioman on Lt. Stitchka's crew in VP-12 at Kaneohe in 1941. Kirk Dunwoody was the AP on our crew and Ens. Fox, who was killed on Dec. 7, was the copilot. I read your article in this last issue of The Scuttlebutt and it brought back a lot of memories.

I received my orders to flight school when we were on Midway, not long after the battle. I have had some questions floating around in my mind for a number of years. Maybe you have some answers.

I remember going out into the hangar shortly after a bomb came thru the overhead. There was smoke everywhere and I was going to the far corner to fire out from between the doors. In the middle of the hangar, deck, in the smoke, was sitting a Chief Ordnance man. He was smoking a cigarette and holding on to one leg, just above the knee. The lower part of the leg was lying to one side, still attached by a strip of skin. He told me that help was coming. Was this Finn?

Shortly after that, I found Stitchka kneeling beside Ens. Fox. He had apparently been killed by the bomb blast. I watched several men lift Chubby Lyons out of the window of the ordnance shop. He had a badly damaged foot and lost it. I saw him a number of years later, somewhere in the world, and he told me he had gotten a prosthetic foot and had re-qualified in carrier aircraft. He found great fun in getting someone to pull his shoe off! When they did it he pressed a spring catch on the brace and they would pull his whole foot off.

I was wondering if you had any idea of what happened to Stitchka. I know where Kirk Dunwoody is. He wrote a couple of years ago and I answered right away, but didn't hear from him again for about a year. He apparently had not received my answer, so I wrote again. Once more, I've heard nothing from him. I know that these little trips down nostalgia lane can be quite trying for some folks.

I had a couple of friends that I'd like to see again. I don't know if you knew them or not. Scotty Nielsen, who was a big blond Swede and a mechanic and there was a radioman by the name of Chatham. I believe Chatham went to flight school. Do you have any info on either of these two people?

I was considering going out to Kaneohe this December, but maybe that wouldn't be such a hot idea. T. Wolfe says that you can't go home again — maybe he was right.

Thank you for a good article, B.J. Miller

As I stated earlier, before World War II, only commissioned officers could be aircraft commanders. NAPs were third pilots and seldom even got to sit in the cockpit. After Pearl Harbor most of the aircraft commanders went to the "nerve center," (we called it the "nervous center"). The cadets and NAPs were made aircraft commanders overnight.

I made Chief Aviation Mechanic in January 1942 and Chief Warrant Officer Patrol Plane Commander in March. These elevations in status were made official before a group of officers in a boardroom without much ceremony or any additional training.

Angie and Joe left for the States in April 1942.

Our squadron patrolled out of Hawaii until the end of May. On one patrol we depth charged a "Japanese submarine" which turned out to be a whale. The mistake was a common one and we later formed a "whale bangers" club.

We slept in what we called the bullpen before our 0400 take off. One morning before a 14-hour-patrol a fellow pilot said he was getting married that Saturday and extended me a special invitation. About midnight that evening, my phone in the BOQ rang. I was asked about the weather conditions in my patrol sector that day, and had I been in contact with the pilot who had invited me to his wedding? He had been patrolling in an adjoining sector. When I said no, they told me that the aircraft and its crew were missing. They were never found.

We'd broken the Japanese code. We knew that the Japanese Fleet was coming, so we loaded up Midway with bombs and torpedoes. I made ferrying trips from Pearl to Midway carrying two 500-pound bombs, or two torpedoes, under the wings of the PBY.

One day, after more than 50 years, I received a telephone call from an ex-cadet Larson. He had read an article I wrote in the Pearl Harbor Survivors History Book and told me he was my PBY navigator when we were ferrying torpedoes to Midway. He said that halfway there we received a message to return to Pearl because Midway was under attack. I told him I didn't remember his name, but I remembered that when patrolling westward out of Midway, we passed over the International Date Line (called the Sunday/Monday line) and I had a crazy navigator who used to send screwy poems and notes up to the cockpit. He said he was that navigator. I asked him if he ever remembered any of the poems and he said he would send me a letter. A copy of the letter follows:

Joe Engel
Pensacola, FL 32507

Dear Joe,

Enclosed find the little 'navigator instructions and another poem. I have some others that I need to get copies of. One starts out:

'Once' when challenged by a fighter, a forlorn and wiry blighter merits of the PBY to name. I surprised my self immensely, as I started out intensely, One by one–their virtue to acclaim.

It's a satisfying feeling when you start down from the ceiling,
Engines out–with ocean all below
You know the crate your gliding will still on top be riding
Not up the creek, no paddles for to row."

I have included a drawing of what I recall the search patterns to be like. This is an idealized situation where 36 planes would search the entire area

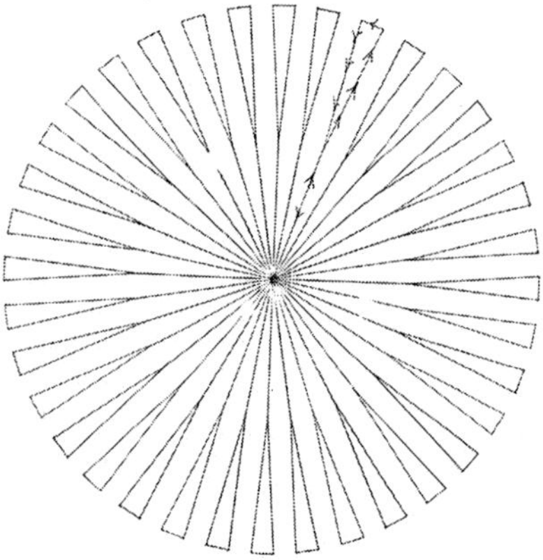

I have some photos of us on Midway that you may not have, as well. Even some of the crazy navigator with the poems.

Glad you are still in good shape. You sounded real healthy and hearty.

'Twas good to talk with you and get a chuckle or two, also

More later…

J. LaMar Larson

I patrolled out of Midway, Canton, Palmyra, and Johnson Islands. On arrival at Johnson Island, we were given a warm reception because the island was so small. When I stopped the aircraft, I saw the Chief that got me out of the Shreveport. La., jail in 1934.

Joe Midway Island

He was a Warrant Machinist and I was an Ensign, so I outranked him. He said. "The next time I see you you'll be Chief of Naval Operations!"

During our leisure time, we reminisced about duty and personnel in the garage in the 1930's.

While patrolling out of Midway I developed an eye infection caused by cigarette smoke in the bomb shelter. The doctor gave me medication and recommended I stop reading. I told him I wasn't reading I was playing chess. When I got well, he challenged me to a game. Later on, I talked him into going on a patrol. I let him sit in the co-pilot's seat on take off and unfortunately, we hit a gooney bird that shattered the windshield on his side. He lost all interest I might have stirred in him for airplane rides after that.

Gooney birds were so huge (40 to 60 lbs.) they had to take off into the wind like aircraft.

The men with nothing else to do used to chase them downwind just to see them spin in. It was interesting to see the ritual they went through when mating, like no other bird.

At Midway PanAm aircraft would land in the lagoon, taxi to the ramp attached to a gasoline tank barge, refuel, and take off for Wake Island and the Orient. The PanAm manager and his family lived on the island. They had a house, a garden, chickens, a cow, and a bull. Whenever the bull performed his family duties, he would fall flat on his face. Everybody on Midway getting orders to go home was warned to "remember the bull!"

American submarines routinely patrolled out of Midway and a submariner jokingly invited me on a patrol. I turned it down, saying it was too dangerous. I returned the offer on one of our patrols and he turned it down for the same reason. I told him, "If you go up with me I know you'll come down, but if I go down with you I don't know if I'll come up!"

In October 1942, I volunteered for a newly organized Aerial Photographic Squadron (VD-1) and was sent back to San Diego. I went to Pensacola on leave to see Angie and Joe and on returning to San Diego, I rented a house and sent for my family.

Our squadron was organized and ready to leave for the South Pacific by March 1943. Angie stayed in San Diego until our second son, Raymond, was born August 2, 1943. Then she returned to Pensacola to await my return.I would not see Raymond for the first time until May 1944, nine months later. This allowed me to join the Stork Club, for men who'd not seen their children yet.

Joe at the Stork Club
** Note signatures on the photo from other fathers who had not yet met their new children*

While in San Diego, we were hurriedly checked out in the B-24 four engine Liberator bombers. We left San Diego in the evening and flew at night to take advantage of celestial navigation.

The night we departed Angie, Joe Junior and my mother-in-law were at the airfield. Just before take-off, Angie realized I had the car keys and sent W.C. Woody, a friend of ours, out to the aircraft. I saw him coming with little Joe Junior struggling to keep up behind him. That image stuck with me all the way to Hawaii. I recalled the incident to Woody years later. He said that he never expected to see me again.

When we departed San Diego, the Navy wrote the aircraft off the books: one dollar for the frame and one dollar for each engine. We fooled them, we brought that plane back!

After 19 hours of flying, my mechanic informed me we were low on fuel. I radioed Hawaii that I was proceeding in directly instead of the route for friendly aircraft. I was given permission and all personnel manned their ditching stations in case I had to make an emergency water landing.

I knew I had some fuel left in the bomb bay tanks before shifting to the mains so I had the mechanic stand by the gas valves in the bomb bay and shift to the bomb bay tanks. As soon as I saw the fuel pressure drop, I had him shift back to the main tanks, providing us with all the fuel in the bomb bay tanks.

Later I found out that the "emergency" wasn't necessary. We had plenty of fuel. The mechanic was also a victim of the short indoctrination period and misread the gauge. Several of our aircraft had the same problem and landed at different airfields.

My landing request to Hawaii approach control included my name. An NAP friend by the name of L.W. Tracy was flying to

Hilo that day and heard my transmission. As soon as he returned from Hilo, he called me at the BOQ and invited me to his place for steaks and drinks. I tried to beg off because I was tired from the 21-hour flight from the States. He wouldn't accept my excuse so I went down and celebrated.

While in Hawaii, we found out that the Japanese were shooting down our Liberators by coming in high at the 10 and two o'clock position because the bow gunner and navigator were operating 30 caliber machine guns out of six universals and they couldn't move the guns fast enough. To counteract this problem we took some hydraulic operated turrets out of the sterns of some flying boats and installed them in the bow of our Liberators. This delayed our departure to the South Pacific by two weeks.

One day the skipper said he was leaving the next day and that I should fly wing on him. On passing over the equator I asked him if he was a "shell back" (one who has crossed the equator before) or a "pollywog" (one who hasn't) He replied that he was a shell back.

My navigator said that we are coming up on Walla Walla and should start our descent. I started down but the skipper kept on going. We were on the ground thirty minutes before he came in, having overshot the island.

Traveling from Walla Walla to Nandi, we lost an engine and had to feather the prop thus causing the aircraft to lose speed. The skipper was nearly out of sight before he got our message because we had to code the message and he had to decode it. He turned around and flew wing on me. I landed at Nandi with no trouble.

The next day the skipper asked if I would fly up to Espirito Santo on three engines. I told him that I could if I unloaded some of my cargo: mail, spare parts, etc. He thought it over and suggested that he could send me an engine or I could lighten the load and proceed on three engines. We decided it was safer to stay on Nandi.

We waited three weeks with no word from the skipper. Eating English lamb and codfish, drinking warm beer, and driving on the left-hand side of the road did not make our stay enjoyable. We finally got a call from Operations that our engine had come in and everyone in the crew helped install it. Were we glad to leave Nandi!

At Espirito Santo, we landed on Marston matting between the palm trees. I looked out the cockpit window and saw my brother-in-law Clifford Johnson. We had a jam session and he asked if I wanted to go cat eye hunting. Cat eyes are very desirable shells from which they make beads. I told him I had to fly to Guadalcanal the next day with some personnel and equipment and I would return the following day for cat eye hunting.

When I flew into the Koli Point, Guadalcanal, airfield they said the skipper wanted to see me. He was in the hospital with malaria as were the other two aircraft commanders. When I arrived at the hospital, he said he had an important mission for me. My co-pilot was to fly my aircraft back to Espirito Santo and the next morning I was to take his aircraft and crew along with a fighter escort to get photos of Munda Airfield on the island of New Georgia.

The next day we took off as planned. The weather was bad and we couldn't find the fighters but proceeded without them. On the first photographic run over Munda Airfield, four anti-aircraft shells hit us. Our aircraft was damaged in the bow, the navigator was wounded, and cabin insulation was all over the cockpit. The crew managed to put a tourniquet on the navigator and give him morphine while I made my second run and proceeded home. On nearing home base, I radioed our difficulty and asked that they meet us with an ambulance, a doctor, and a fire truck.

We landed without incident but found an unexploded shell under my seat. After the shell was defused I wanted it for a souvenir but the skipper got it (it was his aircraft). Rank has its privileges!

The navigator was sent to a hospital in Auckland, New Zealand, and returned to active duty later. Tokyo Rose broadcasted that the Japanese had shot down a B-24 over Munda airfield that day. The "newscast" left me with the eerie feeling that I was listening to my own obituary. I never returned to Espirito Santo.

Aerial photo-reconnaissance played a very important role in World War II. We flew long-range four engine B-24 Liberator bombers. The engines were turbo supercharged, allowing the aircraft to reach an altitude of 30,000 feet. We normally operated between 20 and 30,000 feet. The altitude provided protection from most anti-aircraft fire. The aircraft carried a crew of 11. Our firepower consisted of six 50-caliber machine gun stations, four hydraulic operated turrets and two waist gun stations. In the bomb bays, we had a battery of four cameras equipped with different focal length lenses and we had infrared film available.

We could change the scale of photos by changing altitude or by using a different focal lens camera. Our mission included photographing bombing raids, supply drops to Coast Watchers, bomb damage assessment, photography for the front lines, and mosaic mapping.

Artist rendering of a B-24 Photo Liberator

For night bombing raids and night photography, we carried eight high-powered magnesium photoflash bombs. They were dropped at intervals, using an intervalometer. The bombs were set to explode 2,000 feet above the terrain, lighting up the whole area and tripping the photoelectric cell in the camera thus taking their own pictures. When bracketed by searchlights the cells became inoperative, making it necessary to fly around in the dark until they returned to normal.

On all reconnaissance missions, we had to note the time of day and the altitude when we took photos. The photo interpretation unit could tell the size of a building and how many troops it housed by the length of the shadows, the altitude, and focal length of the camera.

In one instance, we couldn't understand how the Japanese had replaced destroyed aircraft so quickly. There were no shadows and the photos were not taken at noon. It was finally determined that the aircraft were painted on the ground! Another photo showed dead palm trees about the size of a runway. The Japanese had tied the trees together at the top and were building a runway underneath.

The front lines would call us when they ran into difficulty, requesting photos of certain areas. We had the same charts in the aircraft as they had on the ground. We would photograph the area requested, put the film in a small container, attach a small parachute to it and drop it from 100 ft. close to a photo lab trailer behind the front lines. They would review the photos and request air support if necessary.

Sometimes we were told to leave the area in the opposite direction of approaching enemy aircraft (bogies) giving the enemy altitude and heading. After the fighters cleared the area, we were called back to duty.

Mosaic mapping consisted of taking multiple pictures with a fifty percent overlap. Only the center part of the picture could be used because of distortion at the outer edges. The centers of the photos were feather edged and laid out into a complete map. These maps - outlined in detail - the coastal and water topography and were used for amphibious landings.

PBY4 Liberator, Joe and Crew

Luxurious dining, Guadalcanal style

Our main base was at Guadalcanal. We operated from a Marston bomber strip at Koli Point. Our squadron was self-supporting in that we had our own paymaster, commissary officer, doctor, photo lab and photo interpretation unit. When we first arrived, we dug foxholes, erected four-man tents, and put up four- and six-hole privies. We filled our canteens from Lister bags, which were replenished periodically by water trucks. All personnel took half of an Atrabine pill every weekday and a whole one on Sunday to keep from getting malaria. We washed our laundry in the river and our mess hall, was a table in the jungle.

Photo technicians remove camera from a B-24 Liberator upon completion of a reconnaissance mission.

I drew up a plan for a wash and shower room, a mistake, because I soon discovered I had landed the job of building and grounds officer. My working party of enlisted men dug a hole about twenty by twenty feet square and eight feet deep. We filled it with punctured 50-gallon drums and covered it with sandbags and coconut trees. This was our septic tank. Then we got a water purifier to filter the river water and ran it to our shower and washroom. Eventually the Seabees built us a mess hall, sickbay, church, and brig, etc.

A Japanese night bomber (we called him "Washing Machine Charley") paid frequent visits. At first, our only defense was anti-aircraft guns. They always shot behind the target and were not very effective. When we got the night fighters, we saw some action. One of the Japanese planes shot down by the fighters landed right in our campground!

One Sunday an officer drove up in a Jeep and asked if there were any Catholics in camp. I recognized him as a chaplain and I told him there were. He said, "Round 'em up and we'll have Mass." He spread the altar cloth on the Jeep's engine hood and said I could be his altar boy. I told him I didn't know how. He said, "Just do what I tell you." I was checked-out in a hurry!

Joe on the beach at Guadalcanal, 1943

The Seabee Construction Battalion (We called them "Senior Citizens." In my opinion: unsung heroes) built him a Quonset hut church. On Sundays when the church was crowded the chaplain would say, "I see Washing Machine Charley must have come down last night!"

The Coast Watchers were 65 to 70-year-old Aussies and New Zealanders (also unsung heroes) who managed the natives on the coconut plantations on the south Pacific Islands before the war. We put the Coast Watchers and the natives on the islands at night with PBYs and submarines. They had radios and they would keep us informed of Japanese operations. One Coast Watcher had one of his natives working on a Japanese airstrip and the native would keep him informed of the operations.

One day we received a report that 85 aircraft (even detailing the types) were leaving Kahaili Airstrip in Bouganville. It gave us time to get our fighters to altitude over the Russell Islands and get our Liberators out of harm's way in case our defenses were penetrated. The fighters had a turkey shoot!

At one midnight flight briefing we were given the following to obtain night photos of the Army Air Force bombing of Kahaili: maps, weather forecast and codebooks; instructions for finding friendly natives, money, and locations of friendly forces if we were shot down. We signed for morphine serrates (pain killers for wounded crewmen) which had to be returned if not used.

The hardest time during this whole operation was trying to get to sleep after the briefing. You thought about home and your family. After entering your aircraft, you were so busy you didn't have time to worry.

We loaded eight magnesium, very high candlepower, highly explosive photoflash bombs, and fifty caliber machine gun bullets for six twin gun stations.

On take-off, the right main tire failed, causing part of the broken wheel to damage the wing and aileron. We had only one strip and I knew I had to leave the runway, so I ditched the aircraft. We shifted all the bombs and ammunition and had to preflight another aircraft, putting us considerably behind schedule.

After take off, I was pulling a very high power setting trying to get to target on time. I asked my co-pilot to watch the cylinder head temperatures. He said he couldn't see the instruments. I told him to check his oxygen system. Unfortunately, not all aircraft are the same. We were not in our own aircraft and it was nighttime.

A fire broke out in the bow of the aircraft. A hydraulic line had ruptured and sparks from the electric motor ignited the atomized hydraulic fluid. One of the crewmembers put out the fire and I jettisoned the photoflash bombs, aborted the flight, and returned to base. Reports in the morning stated that the first three aircraft were shot down, one plane came back with the lower ball turret, and the crewman shot out. It just wasn't our time on that run. The good Lord had been my co-pilot.

One evening the skipper called me over and introduced me to an Australian Coast Watcher named Wobbie. He said his crew on Bouganville near Kahaili airstrip was out of cigarettes and fuel for their transmitter. He requested we make a drop with these supplies. The skipper asked me to do it, saying we had a drop made up of fuel, cigarettes, and a codebook. The place to drop was close to Khalid near a church. They would put a white cross on the beach for identification.

I was to go in low (50 feet) at dusk. If I had positive identification I was to drop the whole bundle, if I wasn't sure of the location I was to pull the codebook and make the drop. I flew around the area for quite awhile without definite proof and it was getting dark, so I pulled the codebook and made the drop. On arrival back at the base, I found that they received the fuel and were able to relay this information to us.

When Sir Walter Lloyd was researching for his book about the Coast Watchers called Lonely Vigil, our briefing officer, John R. Hubbard referred him to me and I gave him the information and date out of my logbook. He wrote back and said that Wobbie was not at Bouganville at that time. It wasn't until too late that I discovered what he said was true. Wobbie was at our camp when I made that drop. Wobbie later came to our camp, thanked me, and gave me a souvenir but I don't know what happened to it.

Regardless of the weather, Guadalcanal Movie Theater was packed and truly the most popular entertainment on the island.

On 7 December 1943, we were sent to Aukland, New Zealand, for rest and recreation. I rented an automobile that operated on coke; the stove was on the rear bumper. The car had no power and I was stuck in a gutter about four inches deep. An Australian soldier gave the car a little shove and said, "You have a V8 there, Yank!"

When we were ready to return from Tontouta to Espirito Santo, the first aircraft was loaded and could take only half the crew. We decided to stick together and wait for the next aircraft, a wise decision because the first aircraft never got to its destination and they never found out what happened to it.

On returning from seven days R & R at Aukland, New Zealand we had a stop over at New Caladonia. Upon leaving, I had only 5 of my 11 crew members on board an R4D, when the load master said he couldn't take any more passengers, the aircraft was full. I told him that six members of my crew were not aboard. He said, "You'll either have to split your crew or wait until the next aircraft." We got off and waited. That R4D never reached its destination. We lucked out again.

The first two crews (Win Ross' and mine) left Guadalcanal for home in February 1944. Our first stop was Funa Futi. When we departed, the noon flight rations for both crews were all loaded in Win Ross's plane. When they realized the mistake at noontime, they flew up close, indicating that they had all the food. What they didn't know was that we always kept a large can of boneless turkey and crackers aboard for just such an emergency.

The next stop was Palmyra Island then on to NAS Kaneohe Bay, Hawaii. Our orders were to inventory our aircraft and turn them in to Supply. We were to fly home commercial. Before we could leave, we were told to draw the aircraft back out of Supply because we were going to fly them to San Diego. While waiting for weather we played volleyball and Win Ross, who was on my side, broke one of my front teeth with his elbow. We landed in San Diego 16 February 1944.

February 16, 1944, Joe Engel (third from right standing) and his crew landed at North Island, San Diego, after their Guadalcanal tour with Photographic Squadron One.

Chapter Six: East Coast Tours of Duty 1945-1948

I was assigned as Engineering Officer and Flight Instructor with VB4 OTU-2, Jacksonville, Florida. One flight crew crashed, killing all hands, when they attempted to land in inclement weather. On viewing the crash site, I said it couldn't be one of my training crew because they weren't wearing life jackets and parachute harnesses, but I was wrong. They wore the equipment on training flights but were disobeying orders when the instructor wasn't present. I felt really bad about this incident.

While in Jacksonville, we had a hurricane flyaway to Macon, Georgia. My problem was to get enough pilots to fly the aircraft to the hurricane evacuation field as pilots were leaving the service after the war as quickly as they accumulated the necessary points.

I had six fighter and two-transport navigation classroom, aircraft. I led the fighters. I felt I was already out of gas when I took off because the little fighter only held 85 gallons of gasoline. I was used to flying B-24 bombers. We normally landed with 800 gallons of fuel.

Upon arrival over Macon, I gave the signal to break up the formation and operate independently, requesting landing instructions. I was told to orbit. There were two transport aircraft towing two gliders plus yellow training aircraft without radio communication in their pattern. I again requested landing instructions, stating I was low on fuel. Again, I was told to orbit. I finally landed on the grass paralleling but not on the runway. The other fighter aircraft followed me in. It's a miracle there were no accidents.

I called home from the Officers Club to inquire about my family's status. Angie said a tree had just fallen on the house and she was cooking beans on the space heater in the hall.

Six weeks later, I received a call from Macon asking when I was going to pick up the other fighter aircraft. I told them I had all my aircraft. After the second call, I checked and found that a reserve pilot delivered an aircraft to us the day of the evacuation and he was told to take it to Macon. We finally sent a pilot for the aircraft.

In November 1945, the squadron moved to NAS Whiting Field, Milton, Florida. I was Maintenance Officer and Flight Instructor for the four engine PB4Y-2 Privateer bombers. A training crew on the return leg of the final 11-hour navigation flight became disoriented in bad weather and landed on a short grass field in Milton. They were lucky because the field was wet and they plowed one-foot ruts, keeping them from overshooting the field. It took 40 loads of dirt to fill the ruts.

The Training Officer asked me to fly the aircraft back to Whiting Field just a short distance away. I told him I'd look over the situation to see if it was feasible. To take off on this very short dirt field required draining the gas load down to a minimum. In order to turn the aircraft around I had to pull a high power setting, which would damage the light aircraft parked behind me. I requested they move the aircraft. They were reluctant to do this but when I blew some of the sheet metal off the hangars, they were glad they complied.

I made a slow trial run down the runway to see how hard the ground was. Normally we use half flaps for take off, but I selected to start with no flaps until I got the speed, I wanted. I told my co-pilot to give me full flaps - that got us airborne. We just barely cleared the fence at the end of the runway. Most of the airport personnel were betting I wouldn't make it. Every pilot has some hairy flight experiences to tell about.

After reporting to VB-104 at Atlantic City in June 1947, I was told I'd be going to Argentia, Newfoundland, for a three-month tour as Senior Officer of a two-plane detachment after I checked out in the squadron syllabus. I checked the list and found that I was scheduled for low-level training flight with 500-pound live bombs. I contacted the gunnery officer and asked at what level I should drop the bombs, as I had never done any low level bombing. He said 500 feet. I don't know why but I asked, "Isn't that too low?" He said, "You can go higher if you want to."

The procedure was to drop a smoke light in the ocean to be used as a target and a cameraman in the aircraft tunnel hatch would photograph your accuracy. Unfortunately, the ceiling was only 500 feet that day and I thought that if they could drop these bombs at this altitude so could I. The first bomb rocked the aircraft and the plane captain came up to the cockpit and exclaimed. "You nearly lost the photographer out the tunnel hatch, there are holes all over the wings, and it looks like the tires are flat!"

We circled until I found a hole in the overcast and dropped another bomb at 800 feet. The aircraft was rocked again but not as much. Again, I circled and found a hole at 1000 feet and dropped the third bomb, a dud. The last circle took us to 1,200 feet, but the fourth bomb still rocked us a little.

I sent for the ordnance man and asked him if they had always experienced this problem. To my surprise and anger, he stated that they had never dropped live bombs before. Upon returning

I alerted the tower and requested the fire trucks and ambulance be available for the landing. We landed without mishap.

I immediately reported the incident to the Commanding Officer. The accident report reply from the Fleet staff at Norfolk inquired, "if it was old Joe Engel who did such a stupid thing." The Skipper replied that, yes, it was old Joe Engel but that I had been improperly briefed before the flight.

This was the last I heard about the matter but the story didn't end there. After I retired, I was mowing my lawn one day when a stranger stopped and asked if I remembered him and I replied. "No, should I?"

He went on. "Did you drop some bombs in the Atlantic Ocean and nearly blow the aircraft out of the sky?" When I acknowledged the deed, he said he had been my plane captain. I asked him if he ever flew with me again. He said, "No, once was enough."

In July 1947, I was ordered to temporary additional duty as Senior Officer-in-charge of VPB-104, Argentia, Newfoundland, and detachment. The duty was to patrol between Argentia and BW-I in Greenland.

The first order of business was to review a movie of the approach to BW- I that was forty miles up the fiord from BW-3 on the coast. In bad weather, we had to make our let down at BW-3, and then fly up the fiord on visual flight rules. This meant you were in a tunnel with mountains on both sides and overcast for a ceiling. If you couldn't go up the fiord under visual flight rules, you had to fly to the alternate: Goose Bay, Labrador, which was 600 miles away.

There were only two places in the fiord where you could turn around. There was a certain landmark where you lowered your flaps and another where you lowered your landing gear. The wind always blew away from the glacier at BW-1. You landed toward the glacier and took off away from the glacier. This meant you took off downwind. If the wind was over 25 knots, departure had to be delayed.

The personnel at BW-1 were chronically short of small commissary items such as milk, mayonnaise, catsup, etc. The wives would give us (they called us the flyboys) a shopping list and we would shop for them in the Argentia commissary. The Captain had a Lt. (junior grade; jg) for an Executive Officer and this seemed odd to us. They all dressed formally for dinner and that also seemed odd at this remote station.

The Captain asked me to take his uniform to the tailor in Argentia and have stripes put on his coat and have the pants shortened. When I returned the uniform to him, he accepted the work on the coat but said the trousers were too long. I volunteered to take them back but he said I might not return and that he could adjust the trousers. He trusted me with the whole suit but not with the trousers!

I received a teletype message from our skipper in Atlantic City, which stated. "When feasible stage a scouting mission to Frobisher Bay via Fort Chimo and Goose Bay. Find the feasibility of operating in that area, relative to air traffic control, fuel, berthing, and messing facilities."

In July 1947, I left Argentia for Goose Bay on a Saturday and remained overnight. After church on Sunday, I filed a flight plan for Fort Chimo (code name Crystal One), a small outpost where we remained overnight. We slept on cots with brown sheets and after using the privy, which was alongside the cot, you twisted the handle to activate the chemical.

The next morning I filed a flight plan for Frobisher (code name Crystal Two), which was close to the Arctic Circle. According to my clearance and my charts, I was supposed to be flying above the highest terrain. Fortunately, I was flying in clear weather because the mountains were a lot higher than I was flying. Lucked out again!

After landing and getting out of my aircraft, a person grabbed me and ran me into the hangar. He said I'd get frost bitten in that minus 40-degree weather. We purchased a case of beer, opened the window and pushed it into the snow. It appeared that the duty appealed to civilians because of premium pay, gambling, drinking and, oddly enough, outstanding hobby shops.

On preparing for departure the next day we found out we had a severe problem of ice on the wings, almost impossible to remove. I asked if they always had this problem and they said that no one had ever stayed overnight. I thought that it was a fine time to tell me. We removed all the ice but the take off still presented minor problems. The return to Argentia was uneventful.

Our skipper visited us at Argentia and told me that Angie was about to have a baby and that I should be home. I reminded him that I hadn't volunteered for the job and immediately procured my crew's health and pay records for early departure the next day for Atlantic City. When I returned to the Officers Club that evening, the Skipper asked where I had been and I told him I was getting ready to leave the next day. He offered no objections so I carried out my plans.

While I was unpacking my suitcase that evening, I told Angie a joke and she had such a belly laugh she broke her water. We left for the hospital where my son Michael was born August 27, 1947. We told him he was just a big joke. Every woman near delivery who has heard this story wants to hear the joke, but I can't remember it!

The squadron moved to NAS Patuxent River, Maryland, in 1948 and rented one whole block in Lexington Park, a nearby subdivision.

I received dispatch orders from Staff in Norfolk, Virginia, directing me to the Glen L. Martion Aircraft Company in Baltimore to participate in the source coding and provisioning of the new P4-M, the first jet powered seaplane. I spent three weeks with maintenance and supply officers and company personnel on the project. The object of the task was to determine how many and what kinds of parts were needed to support the aircraft, and to indicate the parts that were to be purchased from Glen L. Martion, made at a Navy overhaul depot or bought on the open market.

Naturally, the company had an invested interest in getting as many parts as possible coded in their favor and spent three weeks wining and dining us and offering us tickets to all sorts of shows. I soon grew sick of looking at blueprints and was glad when the task was finally finished. The aircraft was modified to the P6-M and never qualified for production.

Chapter Seven: Photographic School, Pensacola, FL 1949

In 1949, I was transferred to the Naval Air Technical Training Unit (NATTU), Photographic School at Pensacola, Florida. After completing school, I was thinking about asking the school's skipper if I could remain on the school's staff when the phone rang. It was the skipper asking me if I would consider staying on as his operations officer at Chevalier Field when they moved the school to Fort Barrancas.

Photo School graduation, Naval Air Technical Training Unit, Pensacola, Florida, 1949.

NAVY DEPARTMENT, BUREAU OF NAVAL PERSONNEL
SERVICE SCHOOLS
UNITED STATES OF AMERICA
This certifies that
JOSEPH CHARLES ENGEL
has satisfactorily completed the prescribed course of study at the
NAVAL SCHOOL AVIATION PHOTOGRAPHER'S MATE
NAVAL AIR TECHNICAL TRAINING UNIT, NAS, PENSACOLA, FLORIDA
this 9th *day of* DECEMBER 1942
A.D. FRASER, CDR.
U.S. Navy, Commanding

I agreed and asked him what I should do to make the transfer. He suggested I make a request to the Bureau of Aeronautics in Washington, via him, and he would put a favorable endorsement on it. He knew the head man at the bureau so there would be no problem. The request was granted so Angie and I purchased a lot and built a house on Second Street in Pensacola.

We planned a house party to celebrate my 20th anniversary in the Navy and invited the officers of the photo school. Two Naval Academy lieutenants, William McLaughlin and Digger Ferrin (we called him Digger because he had worked in a mortuary before going to the Academy) put on a skit depicting my meeting Angie when I was enlisted.

McLaughlin had on a sailor suit with the pants on backwards and the flap open in the rear. Digger wore a dress. He told my aunt to stop breathing because he could feel the draft. I had given my aunt a camera to take pictures but she forgot to remove the lens cap. McLaughlin retired as a Rear Admiral and I used to kid him that if I had those pictures I'd be drawing his retirement pay.

Whenever Digger got slightly inebriated he would take a woman's hand and tell her that her hands were cold, and had she made any arrangements for a cemetery plot?

Chapter Eight: European Tours 1952-1954

In January 1952 I was transferred to VR-24, Port Lyautey, North Africa. Upon reporting in, I told the Operations Officer I needed flight time for pay purposes. He said he would take care of it. The next day I received a call from Operations: There was a flight going to Lisbon, Portugal and Madrid, Spain, he would schedule me.

On return, I was told to report to the Executive Officer. The XO said. "Engel, you've been in the Navy long enough to know you can't take a flight without notifying the Executive Officer." I replied that this authority is granted to the Operations Officer, who placed me on the schedule. He wouldn't admit this but said there was a flight leaving for Naples, Italy, the next day and he wanted me to take it and look over the place. Naples was cold and dirty and I didn't like what I saw.

As I suspected, I was given a set of orders to report for duty with the VR-24 Naples Detachment. VR-24 Det. was a VIP detachment with a carrier-on-board delivery unit and a post office for mail delivery. It was comprised of 30 officers, 140 enlisted men, one R5D, two R4D-8s and six TBMs.

The detachment was headquartered in a wooden, one-room building. One of the floorboards was missing and a three-legged chair covered the hole. When I reported, I asked for the whereabouts of the Officer of the Day, and was told he had gone to town. I then asked how they got to town. I learned that the detachment rented two taxis by the month and the taxies usually waited outside the front door.

Shortly after reporting to the detachment, I was appointed Operations Officer and, later, Officer-in-Charge.

When I became O-in-C I reviewed our instructions and reports and discovered that many were outdated and no longer relevant and there were duplications and overlaps. My superior didn't seem concerned about the situation so I began submitting wildly fictitious paperwork. After a sufficient time lapse, I again contacted my superior to point out the facts and finally succeeded in adjusting our reporting procedures.

Detachment personnel normally ate breakfast aboard the communications ship in Naples harbor. Lunch was purchased from an Italian vender selling sandwiches. We couldn't drink the water because it was unsanitary so we drank Cokes.

One day I ordered a veal cutlet sandwich and the veal fell on the ground. The vender stooped over, picked up the meat, and put it back in the sandwich. We fired the vendor and chipped in $25 each to buy tables and chairs, and then requested that the Navy furnish us with a cook. That was the start of our cafeteria. We had no barracks so therefore all military personnel were subsisted and lived in hotels or apartments. Later on, a barracks was built.

I began to enjoy the town and benefited by the transfer. The orders to VR-24, Port Lyautey, were not well received by my family for various reasons. It was in the middle of a school year and there was a good deal of uncertainty about living conditions and availability of schools and housing. Many of these problems were solved when I was ordered to Naples.

Hunting for an apartment was a major chore. One of the primary headaches was requirement for a language interpreter. One interpreter said that he had an apartment on the sixth floor of a particular building. I said I didn't want it. He exclaimed that I hadn't even seen it and I replied that I knew I hadn't seen it, but I could smell it!

"Unfurnished" is Italian for no light fixtures or hot water tank. They remove the fixtures and tank to sell on the open market or to the next renter. The electric current is different so you have to get a transformer for every American appliance.

While searching for an apartment, I lived in the Hotel Orient, sharing the room with another naval officer who could speak Italian, a valuable help. I convinced the hotel manager I should get monthly rates, but every month my bill would list daily rates. It would take me an hour to get the bill rectified. I think it was a monthly ritual the manager thoroughly enjoyed.

You didn't dare pull the string over the hotel tub because a maid would be in to wash your back. Maids didn't knock on the door, they just entered. One maid pestered me about needing a senorita. I said I had a senora in the States. She understood that but reasoned that a senora in the States wasn't doing me any good in Naples, Italy.

I told a waiter, who could speak English, that I didn't like the demitasse coffee. He told me to order coffee "latai lunga lunga," meaning a large cup with half milk.

Angie and the children joined me at the end of the school year in June. Life became a lot more enjoyable when my family arrived, but they had to adjust, too.

Our 1952 wooden Chevrolet station wagon presented quite a driving challenge. Naples streets were so narrow that people had to take their chairs indoors so that we could pass. The Italians called all Americans "G.I. Joes" and would call out "Hey, Joe!" when we passed by. My son was tremendously impressed that his old dad had been in Italy only six months and already everybody knew his name!

We lived on the sixth floor of an apartment building on Naples Bay. There were only three other American families in the building. Mike started first grade but it became immediately apparent that he didn't much care for school. He would hide and wait for the school bus to leave, then return to the apartment and claim that he had missed the bus.

His escapades didn't slow down his mastery of the Italian language, however. He came home from school one day bursting to tell his mother the story of Snow White in Italian but she was away from home playing cards so he told the story to the Italian maid. The maid told Angie his Italian story and Angie reported that Mike told the story very well indeed.

I had some battery trouble one day and took Mike along to the store to act as interpreter. The sales people were extremely curious about why he could speak Italian but I couldn't.

Ray also learned some Italian and still uses it occasionally when he's talking to his mother. Joe took accordion lessons but was constantly being scolded by his Italian instructor for not practicing. He still plays (a little!).

I was dispatched to London, England, by Staff at Naples to check out a VR-24 Detachment pilot for Aircraft Commander Status. London had not properly filled out the status change report to Staff requirements. After two check rides, I filled out the necessary forms for the pilot and recommended him for Aircraft Commander.

In 1953, Angie became pregnant with our fourth son, Stephen. I was ordered to ferry an aircraft to Jacksonville, Florida, for overhaul and return a newly overhauled aircraft to Naples.

Angie suggested I contact her sister in Jacksonville for the purpose of buying two dresses. One was an evening dress for New Year's Eve, because the baby wasn't due until after the first of the New Year. Her other request was for watermelons. It was odd shopping for maternity dresses with a woman who wasn't pregnant but the mission was accomplished.

On the return flight, one of my crewmen asked if I had a knife. When I asked him why he wanted a knife, he told me that I wouldn't believe it, but he had found two watermelons behind the rear bulkhead. I explained to him that they were for my pregnant wife and dashed his dreams of a watermelon feast.

We took two vacation trips while in Naples. The first was through northern Italy via Rome, Florence, and Venice, then on through Austria into Germany. We visited many military recreation places in Germany. I remember one in which they had an ice show and one young skater asked where her daddy was while the spot light played across all the bald heads. Five-year-old Michael told her he'd be her daddy and stole the show. After the show, they rolled a wooden floor over the ice and we dined and danced.

The other trip was through the Italian and French Rivera's; Bordeaux, France: Madrid, Valencia, Alacanti, and Barcelona in Spain; then through Nice and Rome to get back home. Angie was pregnant with Stephen and my aunt Lillian, who was visiting from the States, made the trip with us.

Our stay at Lourdes, France, was marred by wet, cold weather but the experience was nonetheless unique. Many French wedding parties visit to have their marriage blessed, and the pilgrims on stretchers and crutches form a procession that seems to stretch for miles. The church has large mosaics of the Holy Rosary mysteries on the ceiling.

We lost a few dollars in Monte Carlo—a hard place to describe! High rollers receive deluxe treatment. Sadly, we didn't fall into the "high roller" category.

A favorite trip was to the Isle of Capri, only an hour-and-a half boat ride from Naples. We visited the monastery vineyards and the Blue Grotto and once spotted King Farouk's yacht in the harbor.

Stephen was born prematurely on November 7, 1953 and weighed less than five pounds, necessitating his stay in the hospital until he reached the magic five-pound weight. Angie never wore her Jacksonville finery and finally gave the dresses away.

Stephen had to be fed every hour when he came home. Angie would remark that I had missed the hourly feedings when I was away on a flight. I told her that maybe I wasn't home, but I was so used to the routine I was awake every hour anyway!

When Stephen was four months old, I suggested that Angie take a 10-day Mediterranean cruise on a Military Service Transport ship. The ship would take her to Tripoli, Athens, Greece, and Istanbul, Turkey. She worried about who was going to care for the baby. I manfully volunteered to take leave and handle the job myself (with the help of the Italian maid).

Angie and baby Stephen in Naples Italy.

On the first day out, I fixed the bottle and pabulum and proceeded to feed Stephen. He started crying when I ran out of pabulum so I grabbed for the bottle without realizing I hadn't screwed the cap on tight. I dumped the whole last bottle of formula all over the baby. I had to bathe the irate Stephen and make new formula. If I could have recalled Angie's ship, I would have!

Angie visited the market place in Tripoli where they still used the barter system and the Parthenon atop the Acropolis in Athens. While in Turkey, the cruise participants were invited to join in the festivities at a Turkish wedding.

The boys and I survived the ordeal but they told their mother that all I fed them was potatoes. Angie proudly presented me with a souvenir from her trip: a meerschaum pipe. I thanked her but was puzzled by her choice because I don't smoke. She knew that, of course, but couldn't resist her "bargain." It was a $9 pipe and she got it for $3. I asked her why she didn't buy two; she could have saved $12!

All Italian apartments had a bidet in the bathroom. Raymond and Joe thought this appliance was an ideal receptacle for their goldfish (who lived on a diet of corn flakes). Raymond decided to take the fish to school for Show and Tell. When the bus driver turned a corner, the bowl overturned. Thinking quickly, he put the fish back into the bowl and got the driver to stop at the next corner water fountain. He recounted his heroics to the class and got an A in Show and Tell.

I was aboard the communications ship in Naples harbor late one evening when I received a telephone call from the squadron to report in as soon as possible. They had an emergency flight to Rhein Main, Germany. I rushed home to pick up the suitcase I always kept packed for such emergencies. When I arrived at the airport, I learned I had a patient aboard in serious condition and someone had already filed my flight plan. Not rechecking the flight plan was a big mistake.

Flying at the required minimum altitude of 17,000 feet over the Brenner Pass I encountered heavy ice buildup on my propellers. Using alcohol as recommended didn't help. I could only maintain a minimum air speed of 80 knots and started losing altitude. My only hope was to break into the clear over the pass and make an emergency landing. As a last resort, I exercised my props by changing rpm, which dislodged the ice with a loud noise when it hit the fuselage. I didn't breathe a sigh of relief until I regained my original altitude.

My next problem was trying to contact Rhein Main radio. I finally received a message from another aircraft, informing me that I was using the wrong frequency. He gave me the correct frequency, which proved to be a lifesaver. When I contacted Rhein Main I learned that I had a head wind 25 knots greater than what I was using and if I'd made my let down with the inaccurate wind information, I would have crashed into the mountains.

The pilot who filed the flight plan had used an outdated Rafax book, which listed the wrong radio frequency for Rhein Main, plus he was given the wrong wind conditions.

As a VIP unit, we flew high-ranking military personnel and elected officials to conferences but we had a few I considered junkets. VIP flying requires the pilot to land the aircraft at the exact time indicated on the flight plan. If you're early, you embarrass the people on the ground and if you're late, you embarrass the people in the aircraft.

I flew an itinerary for the Admiral and his staff from Naples, Italy; to Gibraltar, Spain; and Tripoli, North Africa. I wanted to buy Angie a camel hair coat and myself a pair of Dax slacks in Gibraltar. I knew I had enough time to go into town so I hired a taxi.

When I got back to the airfield, I was confronted by the Admiral's staff commander, yelling that the Admiral had been waiting for me and that I was the worst staff flier he had ever seen. I explained that there was a time differential between Gibraltar and Tripoli and if we left right then we would arrive before our scheduled arrival time but I could leave immediately if the Admiral so desired.

After take off, I contacted Tripoli Airways and tried to get in contact with the Naval Attaché. They said he was on the golf course. I advised the French delegation that we were landing early and requested transportation for the Admiral and his staff. After the Admiral's party left in the small French automobiles, the Naval Attaché arrived and started to scold the Flag Lieutenant for not notifying him. I told him we tried but he was on the golf course. The conversation ended in a draw all around.

One of the Admirals liked to go hunting in Rome. We usually landed in a small dirt field just outside the city. When the grass was very wet and muddy, the aircraft just barely cleared the treetops on take off the Staff Commander wanted to know if we always got that close to the trees. I told him I thought it was a dangerous operation and I didn't think the Admiral should use that particular field. He said, "Write a letter stating that fact."

I related the incident to my superior and he said he would look into the matter. The next day he called and told me to go ahead with the letter. I outlined the danger of the operation and further stated that I knew the Italians used the field but their safety factor was a lot lower than ours was. I recommended that we discontinue use of the field. I wish I had saved the letter because written across the front in pencil: "OK" (signed the Admiral).

I flew another Admiral down to Bahrain Island to relieve the Admiral stationed there. On the way down the pipeline in the desert, the aircraft developed a propeller oil leak. I contacted Baghdad, Iraq, flight control and requested the Naval Attaché provide maintenance help, I sat in the cockpit while the repair was being accomplished, and Iraq's 18-year-old Prince arrived and I photographed all the pomp and polish of the welcoming ceremonies. Thirty days later, they assassinated him. While in Bahrain we visited Saudi Arabia and bought copper slipper ashtrays (which we could have purchased for half the price at home).

An Italian Admiral on board one conference flight asked me for the loan of a dollar and paid me back a short time later. I had hoped he would forget about repaying me so that I could always say that an Italian Admiral owed me a dollar.

On another flight, I was ordered to pick up Danny Kaye and his USO troupe at Pisa. The weather was bad and on approach I contacted approach control and told them I was estimating over Pisa at 45 (45 minutes after the hour), flying at 9,000 feet, and requested let down instructions. Normally (in the States) there would be a slight pause while they checked for other aircraft in the area. Not at Pisa! They immediately gave me clearance to let down. A panicked commercial airliner radioed that they were estimating over Pisa at 48 and flying at 9,000 feet. They requested that we descend to 8,000 and stand by on the frequency until they were clear. We had to make our own clearances!

When we left Pisa, the weather was still bad and Danny Kaye and the troupe got sick. We were diverted to Rome because the weather was so bad at Naples that one aircraft had crashed into the mountains and another on the runway. They would advise us when the runway was cleared. I gave the USO troupe the option of going to a hotel or waiting for the runway to clear. They decided to wait and we left Rome at the first opportunity.

Nobody expected us at Naples that night so I had to arrange for transportation and hotel accommodations for the troupe. When I arrived home in the early morning hours Angie was surprised to see me because they had told her I would be staying overnight in Rome.

During the 1953 Suez Canal discussions, I was ordered to take a group of high-ranking military officers to Saudi Arabia for a conference relative to the canal. Everybody in the squadron wanted me to bring them a camel saddle when they heard about the trip. Just before departure, the Operations Officer decided I couldn't leave because they hadn't received my diplomatic clearance but the military party I was flying insisted that I go. I said that since I had to refuel at Athens, Greece, I would get the clearance there.

Immediately after take off I contacted Saudi Arabia Flight Control and requested they contact the Naval Attaché to procure the diplomatic clearance. I lost contact with Flight Control shortly after the transmission. While refueling I tried to make contact with Saudi Arabia again with no results. Athens Operations wouldn't clear me until I promised that if I didn't obtain diplomatic clearance by the time I reached the halfway point between Athens and Saudi Arabia, I would return to Athens. Fortunately, I got the clearance in time.

I was sitting in a taxi at a traffic light in Saudi Arabia when an Arab threw three fez's and three elephant ivory shoehorns into the cab. I threw them out. He threw them back. The taxi driver said that the fellow wanted to sell them to me, so I tossed out a couple of dollars. The Arab bowed at the waist and a sale was made.

I was ordered to return to Naples without the passengers, as the conference was to be too lengthy to wait.

The whole crew purchased Arabian dress and suggested we wear them on arrival at Naples that night. We not only surprised the Italian customs but my family as well. For some reason Angie had brought the children to the airport to meet the aircraft. Oh, yes, everybody got their camel saddles.

On completion of my tour of duty in Naples, I requested commercial ship transportation back to the States. We were scheduled aboard the USS Constitution. It took ten days to reach New York from Genoa, Italy via Gibraltar.

Angie, Ray, Mike, Stephen, and I had one stateroom while Joe Junior was placed with some other military dependent children in another room. Stephen was still on formula and baby food, which was furnished by the ship. It wasn't difficult to keep track of the children. They could always be found at the ship's movie.

On the evening scheduled for the Captain's dinner there was to be dancing and games to follow. When I got back to the stateroom after the dinner I found my wife's formal thrown over a chair and her in bed. Poor Angie was seasick and told me I would have to attend the dancing and games alone but I decided not to go.

In July 1954, I was transferred to the Naval Air Rework Facility at NAS Pensacola as Production Engineering Officer. The job required many trips to Washington D.C., requesting new machinery and updating facilities. Bureaucracy is a classic problem and it was hard to get anything accomplished. I did, however, enjoy test flying the overhauled aircraft and living in Pensacola, Angie's hometown. I made Commander on this assignment.

Chapter Nine: Back to the East Coast 1957-1961

In June 1957, I was transferred to the Military Air Transport Squadron at McGuire AFB, Trenton, N.J. as Maintenance Officer and line pilot. I checked out in the R6D and C-118 aircraft (both the same plane, one Navy and the other Air Force).

The check-out involved learning all the aircraft systems: fuel, electronic and hydraulic, and weight and balance requirements for cargo loads. To be an Aircraft Commander Line pilot you had to demonstrate your ability to fly in adverse conditions such as bad weather, engine failure and various emergencies. This is accomplished by both actual flying demonstrations and sessions in the simulator. You also had to fly several trips as co-pilot before being designated.

We had to check in at Operations two hours before each flight. The time was spent checking the weather, reading Notams (notice to airman) for the route, flight checking the aircraft, and briefing the crew as to their duties and responsibilities. (There was a different crew on each flight, some Navy and some Air Force.)

The aircraft carried 66 passengers or 20,000 pounds of cargo. If you carried passengers, you departed from McGuire A.F.B. If you carried cargo, you flew to Dover, Delaware. We refueled at St. John's, Newfoundland, and again at Lages in the Azores, en route to Rhein Mien, Germany; Chateauroux, France, Mendenhall, England, or Rota, Spain. It took five hours from McGuire to St. John's, nine hours to the Azores, and five hours to the continent. On arrival, the aircraft was unloaded and reloaded. The same crew returned the aircraft to McGuire after a one day layover.

On one flight I lost power on one engine going into Lages and had to feather the propeller (turn the propeller blades for less drag) and cut the engine. I needed an engine change and the aircraft wouldn't be available for flight test until 1600 the following day.

At 1000 the next morning, I obtained transportation to the maintenance hangar to check on the progress being made. They said the aircraft was ready for test flight. I asked if the cargo had been unloaded, and they assured me it had been. I rounded up my crew and made the test flight, which was acceptable.

When I filed my flight plan I noticed that my weight and balance form indicated the aircraft was grossed at 105,000 pounds of which 17,000 pounds was cargo. I questioned this because I had left Dover with 20,000 pounds of cargo. The loading crew said Dover must have short loaded us and I asked if they checked the belly compartment. It had 3,000 pounds in it, which they had overlooked, which meant I was 3,000 pounds overweight. Instead of draining 3,000 pounds of fuel, they removed 3,000 pounds of high priority cargo from the main cabin and left the low priority cargo in the belly!

On another flight to Europe, we were diverted to Goose Bay, Labrador, because St. John's was closed due to blowing snow. At departure time my flight attendant said two of my 66 passengers were missing, were we going to leave? I said no I wouldn't leave anyone in this cold country. I called the tower and stated my problem. The flight attendant then sheepishly reported that the "missing passengers" had been found in bassinets, under the seats.

While at McGuire, we lived in a subdivision in Yardville, New Jersey. None of the neighbors knew each other so we started a tradition of periodic house parties at various homes. The group decided that we should all go to Mama Leone's Italian restaurant in New York City as a special excursion. By the time the appointed evening arrived, everyone had cancelled but I told Angie I was all fired up and we were going anyway.

Now, I'll be the first to admit that my strong suit is stick-to-it-iveness but my weak point is waiting in line. The restaurant was crowded when we arrived and I was prepared to give the project up but Angie persuaded me to have a little patience. Sure enough, in about 10 minutes we were seated for a wonderful interlude of wine, antipasto and many courses of food, a delightful meal!

Radio City was within walking distance and Angie wanted to take the opportunity to see a show. Again there was a line, again Angie persuaded me, again we were seated and enjoying ourselves after a very short wait. Well after midnight I drove home on the freeway while Angie dozed - impatient for the next day when I could tell the neighbors all about the great evening they had missed.

In 1959, I was transferred back to the Naval Air Rework Facility at NAS Pensacola as Aeronautical Engineering Officer, Quality Control and test pilot. This meant recommending aircraft changes to the Bureau of Aeronautics including flight safety and efficiency improvement. We also developed ultrasonic cleaning of aircraft parts, reclaiming oil by centrifugal force, and test flying overhauled aircraft.

R5D-3 Transport by Douglas

UF-1 Albatross Amphibian by Grumman

R6D Transport by Douglas

TV-2 Two Seat Jet by Lockheed

I retired from the Navy in 1961 after more than 30 years service and more than 10,000 flying hours.

Flight of the Silver Eagle
Petty Officer 1937
Chief Petty Officer 1941
Warrant Officer 1942
Commander 1954

Naval Aviation Pilot Profile

2/31 ENLISTED U.S. NAVY
6/31 AVIATION MECHANICS SCHOOL
1935 NAS PENSACOLA FL
1937 FLIGHT CLASS
1938 VP-7 SAN DIEGO CA
1938 VP-8 HONOLULU OAHU
1938 VP-24 NAS KENEOHE OAHU
1942 PHOTO SQUADRON ONE QUADALCANAL
1944 TRAINING SQUADRON JACKSONVILLE FL
1947 VP-24 ATLANTIC CITY NJ
1949 PHOTO SCHOOL PENSACOLA FL
1952 VR-24 NAPLES ITALY
1954 NARF PENSACOLA FL
1957 VR6 MC GUIRE AFB TRENTON NJ
1959 NARF PENSACOLA FL
1961 RETIRED

AWARDS

DFC, AIR MEDAL, NAVY UNIT COMMENDATION, GOOD CONDUCT MEDAL, AMERICAN DEFENCE SERVICE MEDAL, AISATIC PACIFIC CAMPAIGN MEDAL, WW2 VICTORY MEDAL, NAVY OCCUPATION MEDAL.

Epilogue: 1962 - 1986

When son Mike attended St. Bernard College in Cullman, Alabama, he worked for National Rent-A-Car. Whenever they had a car or truck in that area, which had to be returned to Pensacola, they called on Mike. He could get home for the weekend and get paid for the trip. One evening Joe Junior called with the news that number three son was in jail in Alabama, needed $35 for the speeding fine, and that Western Union was closed. I thought that a night in jail wouldn't be too harmful, but Angie took quite the opposite view! She insisted that she call the sheriff to discuss the matter.

I wired Mike the money the next morning. When he got home, he said that his mother's phone call must have done some good because that morning the sheriff had taken Mike to his house where the sheriff's wife cooked them breakfast.

In 1962, I went to work for the Florida National Bank as Manager of the bank facility at the Naval Air Station and in 1963, I became manager of Pen Air Credit Union.

Back in the days when Catholics weren't supposed to eat meat on Fridays' I came home from the credit union for lunch when Angie was away. I rummaged through the cabinets for a can of tuna but couldn't find any "tuna" so I settled for a cheese sandwich. Angie came in and was startled because I never eat cheese. I self-importantly retorted that I wouldn't be eating cheese if she kept tuna in the house. All I had been able to find were five cans of "chicken." She pointed out that the five cans in dispute were "Chicken of the Sea" tuna. Angie's right. I don't know a thing about the kitchen. One thing I do know, I attribute a long and happy life to Angie's olive oil and garlic seasoning!

In 1966, we purchased a lot in the Seaglades subdivision on Grand Lagoon. Perdido Key, and built a house.

A yearly tradition at our house is the New Year's Eve party. One year we were having drinks in the front bedroom when I noticed a drawer open in the built-in dresser. I closed it. A few minutes later, I noticed that it was open again. I was ready to take the pledge until I realized that the children in the adjoining room were pushing the drawer open from the other side. I retired permanently in 1973. My hobbies are golf and sailing.

In December 1986, we returned to Pearl Harbor to celebrate the 45th anniversary of the December 7th bombing and our 50th wedding anniversary. We stayed at the Hale Koa military hotel and enjoyed seven days of sightseeing, including a visit to NAS Kanoeohe (which now accommodates 10,000 Marines), and the Don Ho show and Hawaiian luau. Don Ho had learned that we were celebrating our anniversary and had us perform with him on stage. He joked that Catholics have rhythm and bingo. If rhythm doesn't work, bingo! He singled out a couple who had been honeymooning in Hawaii for six days: "One more day and you be weak!" he said.

The eight-hour, red eye flight from Hawaii to Dallas was tiresome. The attendants frequently served drinks and peanuts to keep us occupied and I told Angie that if I ate any more nuts I'd go nutty. I went to the restroom and while I was washing my hands, I caught sight of a man out of the corner of my eye. It startled me as I thought I had locked the door. I turned, exclaiming. "How did you get in here!" only to discover I was talking to myself. The stainless steel bulkhead was reflecting my own image. On the way back to my seat, I encountered an attendant wearing earrings that glowed in the dark. I joked that

I would like to talk her out of them and she said she would give them to me if I would wear them. I agreed but I'll bet everyone on the plane thought I was from San Francisco! I told Angie about my experience in the head and she said that I really must be a "nutty old man."

Joe and Angie with Don Ho in Hawaii 1986

Maybe she was right! I recall meeting an elderly gentleman from Gadsden, Alabama, one day when I was visiting the Naval Aviation Museum and asked him to do me a favor. When I last had contact with my Navy shipmate Win Ross, he had left the Navy and set up an optometry practice in Gadsden. I asked the gentleman if he knew Win? He told me that Win had made the glasses he was wearing but it had been a long time ago and he wasn't sure if Win was still alive or not.

I asked the gentleman for his name and phone number and he told me he was Robert E. Lee. He had flown his plane from Gadsden to Pensacola. His apparent age prompted me to ask about his pilot's license. He didn't have one but did file a flight plan. I kept myself busy trying to figure out how I would explain to Angie that I was late getting home because I had been talking to Robert E. Lee. I called Mr. Lee a few days later and learned that Win Ross had indeed died and that his wife had remarried.

Joe and Angie celebrate their 50th Wedding Anniversary in Pensacola, FL by renewing their wedding vows at St. Michael's Church, the same church they got married in 1937

Flight of the Silver Eagle
Pensacola, FL 1986 - 2007

This Autobiography was originally written during the 1980's and distributed to my immediate family after our 50th wedding anniversary in 1987. Since then Angie and I have continued to enjoy our family, Holy Spirit our Catholic Parish, the Silver Eagle Association, the Pearl Harbor Association and living in Pensacola. We have four Sons, ten Grandchildren, and six Great Grandchildren.

In 2004, hurricane IVAN destroyed the house we had lived in for 40 years. We saved my flight logs, original autobiography paperwork, computer, and a few other items that we were able to bring with us the night before the storm.

A few weeks after IVAN, Angie and I were living with our son Ray and his wife Debbie. I remember thinking: We survived the Depression, Pearl Harbor, World War II, and now IVAN. It's part of our journey.

Angie and I will celebrate our 70th wedding anniversary together on February 6th 2007. We are blessed.

Joe and Angie
Memorial Day2006

NAS Pensacola - Naval Air Museum - exhibits planes *<u>flown by CDR Engel as a Silver Eagle</u>*

I flew the Grumman F8F-2P Bearcat (left picture above) that was used for photographic-reconnaissance training in Pensacola in 1949. The bureau number is 121710 and it is one of only 60 built. The Bearcat was also the last propeller-driven aircraft flown by the Blue Angels. Maximum Speed: 447 M.P.H. at 28,000 ft.; Service Ceiling: 40,700 ft.; Range: 865 miles.

The R4D-8 traveled reliably over water and in areas with few or no navigation aids or accurate maps. They survived in every environment from the heat of Africa to the cold of Alaska, flying in all types of weather. I flew the plane (left picture above) 46 times for 146 hours in Europe in 1952 and 1953. These planes were attractive because of their large load-carrying capacity. Crew: Three; Capacity: 27 passengers, 10,000 lb cargo. Speed: Max 227 mph; Range:1,975 miles.

Flight of the Silver Eagle

CDR Joseph C. Engel, USN Ret.

Joe's "Butch" PBY4 Liberator -center
Planes shown in order of flight - left to right.

FLIGHT of the Silver Eagle by Joe Engel, SR

Flight of the Silver Eagle is a mini-autobiography of Joe Engel's military career as well as the story of his growing family, published by Patriot Media, Inc., Niceville, Florida.

Joe started his military career by enlisting in the Navy in 1931 and received his pilot flight training in 1937. His exotic assignments carried him throughout the world and while on active duty, he flew over two-dozen types of aircraft and logged over 10,000 flying hours. Two of the actual aircraft flown by Joe Engel, a F8F Grumman Bearcat Fleet Photo Trainer and a BU No. 50821 Douglas Twin Engine Transport, now reside in the Naval Air Station Museum at Pensacola, Florida.

CDR Engel's book may be ordered by credit card at the Patriot Media Publishing web site: www.patriotmediapublishing.com or by sending a check for total amount and a letter or copy of this order form to:

Patriot Media, Inc.
Flight of the Silver Eagle
PO Box 5414
Niceville, FL 32578.
www.patriotmediainc.com

ISBN-13: 978-0-9791642-0-0
ISBN-10: 0-9791642-0-6
51195
9 780979 164200

Check if you are, or you're related to, a Silver Eagle_

Name:_______________________________________
Address:_____________________________________
City:_________________________State_________
Zip Code:________Phone Number:______________

Copies ordered:__________ *Total enclosed:______
*Orders shipped outside the US or
Canada add shipping charges of $1.00 per item.

Enclose a check for the total amount with order form.
Include $11.95 and $3.00 per item *shipping and handling* for a total of $14.95 per copy.

Florida Residents add 6% sales tax of $.72 a copy.
Thank you for your purchases. We hope you enjoy
Flight of the Silver Eagle, By CDR Joseph C. Engel USN Ret.